D0268935

941·08

This book is to be returned on or before
the last date stamped below. £5·25

0007 635

THE AGE OF REFORM

1820-1850

Vyvyen Brendon

Hodder & Stoughton

A MEMBER OF THE HODDER HEADLINE GROUP

ACKNOWLEDGEMENTS

The publishers wish to thank the following for permission to reproduce illustrations in this volume:
Cover – Thomas Armstrong: 'Manchester and Salford Children' © Manchester City Art Galleries;
Mary Evans Picture Library p25; Punch Publications p37; Mary Evans Picture Library p56;
Hulton-Deutsch Collection p65; The Mansell Collection p79; Punch Publications p90; Mary Evans
Picture Library p97.

The publishers also wish to thank the following for their permission to reproduce material in this
volume:
Cambridge University Press for the extracts from JCD Clark, *English Society 1688-1832* (1985);
VAC Gatrell, 'Crime, Authority and the Policeman-state', *Cambridge Social History of Britain*, vol.3
(1990); FML Thompson, 'A Percentage of the population of England and Wales living in towns',
Cambridge Social History of Britain (1990); J Obelkevich, *Cambridge Social History of Britain* (1990); *The
Independent on Sunday* for the extract from 'More Modern than we are' by R Foster, IOS 4/7/93;
Longman Group UK for the extracts from A Biggs, *The Age of Improvement* (1979 edn) and C Emsley,
Crime and Society in England 1750-1900 (1987); Methuen & Co for the extract from AJ Taylor (ed), *The
Standard of Living in Britain in the Industrial Revolution* (1975); extracts from P Mandler, *Aristocratic
Government in an Age of Reform* (1990) by permission of Oxford University Press; Routledge for the
extracts from J Burnett, *Useful Toil* (1974); G Kitson Clark, *The Making of Victorian England* (1962);
University of Wales Press for the extract from N McCord, 'Some Limitations of the Age of Reform'
in *British Government and Administration*, H Hearder & D Loyn (eds) (1974); Victor Gollancz for the
extracts from Edward Thompson, *The Making of the English Working Class* (1963).

Every effort has been made to trace and acknowledge ownership of copyright. The publishers will be
glad to make suitable arrangements with any copyright holders whom it has not been possible to
contact.

Author's Acknowledgements

I am grateful to St. Mary's School, Cambridge for giving me the opportunity to take up a
Schoolteacher-Fellowship at St. Peter's College, Oxford and to the Master and Fellows of
St. Peter's for their help and hospitality.

British Library Cataloguing in Publication Data
A catalogue for this book is available from the British Library.

ISBN 0 340 591927

First published 1994
Impression number 10 9 8 7 6 5 4 3 2 1
Year   1998 1997 1996 1995 1994

Copyright © 1994 Vyvyen Brendon

All rights reserved. No part of this publication may be reproduced or
transmitted in any form or by any means, electronic or mechanical,
including photocopy, recording, or any information storage and
retrieval system, without permission in writing from the publisher or
under licence from the Copyright Licensing Agency Limited. Further
details of such licences (for reprographic reproduction) may be
obtained from the Copyright Licensing Agency Limited, of
90 Tottenham Court Road, London W1P 9HE.

Typeset by Litho Link Ltd, Welshpool, Powys, Wales.
Printed in Great Britain for Hodder & Stoughton Educational,
a division of Hodder Headline PLC, 338 Euston Road, London
NW1 3BH by Page Bros (Norwich) Ltd.

CONTENTS

Approaching Source-based Questions   1
Introduction   4
1 Changing Times   9
2 Altering the Constitution   18
3 Saving the Church   28
4 Disciplining Paupers   38
5 Punishing Felons   49
6 Educating the Poor   60
7 Controlling the Workplace   72
8 Sanitising Towns   82
9 Freeing Trade   92
10 Judging the Age of Reform - The Historical Debate   102
11 Dealing with Examination Questions   111
    Specimen Answers to Source-based Questions   111
    Preparing Essay Answers   114
    Possible Essay Titles   115
    Specimen Essay Answer   119
Bibliography   122
Index   124

APPROACHING SOURCE-BASED
QUESTIONS

Source-based questions have become an important part of History examinations at all levels in recent years. Students who have studied History at GCSE and Standard Grade level will be used to handling various types of sources. The skills they have learned in handling evidence will continue to be applicable at a more advanced level, but there will be more sophisticated skills to master and the sources themselves may be more demanding.

During your studies you will encounter both primary and secondary historical evidence. The distinction between the two is sometimes artificially exaggerated: all sources have their value and limitations, and it is possible to worry unnecessarily about a 'hierarchy of sources'. The important thing for the student is to feel confident in handling all sources. The majority of sources in this book are primary sources, since they are the raw material from which historians work. Many are of a documentary nature, since that is the type most commonly found in examinations. However, there are also statistics and many examples of visual evidence. The comments below will usually apply to *all* types of evidence.

When a student is faced with a piece of historical evidence, there are certain questions that he or she should always ask of that source; but in an examination that student will be asked specific questions set by an examiner and, in the light of pressures, not least of which is time, it is important to approach these questions in an organised and coherent fashion.

The following advice should be borne in mind when answering source-based questions. Some of the advice may appear obvious in the cold light of day but, as examiners will testify, the obvious is often ignored in the cauldron of the examination room!

1 Read the sources carefully before attempting to answer the questions, whether there is one source or a collection of them. This will give you an overview of the sources which will usually be connected and related to a particular theme. You will study the individual sources in detail when you answer specific questions.

2 Always look carefully at the attribution of the sources: the author and date of publication; the recipient, if any; the context in which the source was produced. All these will often give you an insight in addition to that provided by the content of the source itself.

3 Mark allocations are usually given at the end of each question or sub-

question. Ignore the marks at your peril! The number of marks will almost certainly give you some indication of the length of answer expected. Length of answer is not an indicator of quality, and there is no such thing as a standard answer but it is commonplace for candidates in examinations to write paragraph-length answers to questions carrying one or two marks. A question carrying such a low mark can usually be adequately answered in two or three sentences. You do not have the time to waste your purple prose in examinations! Similarly, a mark allocation of nine or ten marks indicates the expectation of a reasonably substantial answer.

4 Study the wording of the questions very carefully. Some questions will ask you to use *only* your own knowledge in the answer; some will ask you to use *both* your own knowlege *and* the source(s); some will insist that you confine your answer to knowledge gleaned from the source(s) *alone*. If you ignore the instructions, you will certainly deprive yourself of marks.

5 If there are several sources to be consulted, ensure that you make use of the ones to which you are directed – candidates have been known to ignore some or choose the wrong ones!

6 Certain types of question require a particular type of response:
a) Comparison and/or contrasting of sources: ensure that you do consider all the sources referred to in the question.
b) Testing the usefulness and limitations of sources: if you are asked to do both, ensure that you do consider both aspects. You may be required to evaluate a source in relation to other information provided, or in the context of your own background knowledge of the subject.
c) Testing reliability. This is not the same as considering the utility of a source, although students sometimes confuse the two concepts.
d) Phrases such as 'Comment upon', 'Analyse' or 'Assess'. Ensure that you do what is asked. Do not be afraid of quoting extracts from a source in your answer, but avoid over-quotation or too much direct paraphrasing. Questions will usually, although not always, be testing more than comprehension, and therefore you should be illustrating or amplifying a particular point. Always *use* the sources and do not just regurgitate what is in front of you.
e) Synthesis: this is a high level skill which requires you to blend several pieces of evidence and draw general conclusions.

7 If at all possible, avoid spending too much time on the sources questions in examinations. Frequently candidates answer the sources questions thoroughly but do not allow themselves enough time to do justice to the rest of the examination paper, and essay answers sometimes suffer in consequence if they are attempted last.

8 If possible, read published examiners' reports which will give you further indication as to the most useful approaches to particular questions, and the pitfalls to avoid.

A Note on this Collection of Sources

It is the intention of this collection to give ideas to teachers and realistic examples of sources and questions to students, either for use in schools and colleges or for self-study purposes. However, they are intended to be flexible. If it is found helpful, adapt the questions or mark allocations, or devise new questions; or use the sources as part of coursework or personal studies. You might even find it an interesting exercise to put together your own sources and appropriate questions!

BARNFIELD COLLEGE LIBRARY ROTHERHAM AVENUE

INTRODUCTION

The first half of the 19th century was a time of unusually rapid change. Economic change was so convulsive that the term 'Industrial Revolution' was coined to characterise it, though historians still debate whether that phrase is appropriate to describe the new manufacturing techniques and forms of transport. Social change produced a more urban and class-conscious Britain, which is reflected in the writing of contemporary poets, novelists and commentators (Chapter 1). Political change occurred largely because individuals and popular movements drew parliament's attention to the urgent problems of a society in transition and to the need for reform. The purpose of this book is to illustrate, through a wide variety of sources, the responses of governments and people to these momentous changes. The chapters deal with separate developments, such as disciplining paupers, controlling the workplace and sanitising towns, and often pose the question of whether 'reform' actually made things better. These themes can be understood only within the context of the political narrative set out in this introduction.

In 1820 the Tories still enjoyed the virtual monopoly of power which had been theirs since before the French wars (1793–1815), through which William Pitt the Younger and Lord Liverpool had successfully led the country. The Tory party was identified with unflinching opposition to revolutionary France and with staunch defence of the Established Church of England and the British Constitution – hence their toast of 'Church and King'. In the years immediately following victory at Waterloo in 1815 Tory policies had been largely reactionary: they defended the interests of the country gentry through the Corn Law and the abolition of income tax (Chapter 9), and repressed the growing agitation for parliamentary reform by the use of spies, troops and laws.

During the more peaceful 1820s, as younger men with less vivid memories of the French Revolution came into the cabinet, the Tories began to adopt more liberal policies. In 1824 they repealed the Combination Acts, which Pitt had passed at the height of the French wars to prevent the development of trade unions. Trade was freed from some of its many restrictions (Chapter 9). The Home Secretary, Robert Peel, reformed the penal code and the prisons, as well as establishing the Metropolitan Police force (Chapter 5). There were even cabinet ministers (such as the Foreign Secretary, George Canning) who believed in granting political rights to those who did not belong to the Church of England – Dissenters and Roman Catholics. Most Tories found this unthinkable until Daniel O'Connell's Catholic Association threatened the peace of the kingdom in 1828. By then Liverpool had resigned after suffering a stroke and Canning was dead; it was the hero of Waterloo, the Duke of Wellington, who reluctantly led the Tories to repeal the laws against Protestant Dissenters and, in 1829, the laws against Roman Catholics (Chapter 3). Disastrously divided by this breach in the 'unalterable constitution' but hostile (for the most part) to the further changes demanded by the revived parliamentary reform movement, the Tories lost seats in the general election of 1830 and had to give way to the Whigs at the end of the year.

At their political banquets the Whig leaders (aristocratic heirs of Pitt's rival, Charles James Fox) toasted 'Civil and Religious Liberty all over the World'. The new Prime Minister, Lord Grey, had for some time believed in a moderate measure of parliamentary reform and was thus able to meet popular demand half-way with the Reform Act of 1832 (Chapter 2). Confirmed in power by a general election at the end of that year, the Whigs passed further cautious reforms dealing with some of the problems of the day: the lax state of the Church (Chapter 3), the expense of poor relief (Chapter 4), the continuing harshness of the penal code (Chapter 5), the lack of education for the masses (Chapter 6), the appalling conditions in factories (Chapter 7) and the outdated running of towns (Chapter 8). Under the leadership of Grey's successor, Lord Melbourne, the Whigs failed to address the deteriorating conditions caused by a serious trade depression in the late 1830s. The establishment of pressure groups such as the campaign against the new Poor Law, the Ten Hours movement, the anti-Corn Law League and Chartism suggests that the Whigs had by no means satisfied the demand for reform.

Meanwhile, Peel had assumed the leadership of the Tory party. He had served for a few months as Prime Minister in 1834–5, after the Whigs resigned over the delicate issue of the Irish church. But, despite Peel's acceptance of parliamentary reform in the Tamworth Manifesto, the Tories did not win enough seats to continue in government in 1835. Faced with difficulties both inside and outside parliament, the Whigs struggled on until 1841 when the mounting government deficit forced them from office. Though the Tory victory in the general election of that year cannot entirely be ascribed to a 'new Conservatism', Peel's government did from the first take steps to modernise trade and industry. The Bank Charter Act and the Companies Act stabilised, and restored confidence in, economic institutions. Together with the free trade budgets of 1842 and 1845 and the re-introduction of income tax, these measures helped to bring the recession to an end and thus to increase general prosperity (Chapter 9). Peel was so convinced that his economic policies were the best means of improving working-class life, that he was reluctant to undertake extensive social reform. Nevertheless, the shocking revelations in new reports on living and working conditions pushed the government into passing the Mines Act and a further Factory Act (Chapter 7) and into considering a measure of public health reform (Chapter 8).

Preoccupied as both Tories and Whigs were with the 'Condition of England question' (as writers called the plight of the poor), they had not faced up to the even more serious condition of Ireland. In spite of Roman Catholic Emancipation, religious grievances still rankled there (Chapter 3) and were not diminished by the increased government grant to the Maynooth Roman Catholic seminary in 1845. Meanwhile, a Royal Commission on land occupation had recommended moderate measures to relieve the acute poverty and insecurity of Irish peasants; but the subsequent bill had been withdrawn for amendment after opposition in the Lords. At this point the failure of the 1845 potato crop intensified Irish destitution – and also threw the political scene into confusion by bringing to the fore the already contentious issue of the Corn Laws. Peel's dramatic response, removing duties on corn against the will and the votes of most of his party, led to his resignation in 1846 (Chapter 9).

The popular hero-worship of Peel which resulted from his political martyrdom was augmented by his tragic death in 1850. But Conservatives blamed him for the disastrous split in the party, which did not win a parliamentary majority again until 1874. Peel's own adherents, the 'Peelites', drifted as a leaderless group in parliament until most of them (including W. E. Gladstone) merged with the Whigs in the late 1850s to form the Liberal party.

Before that, in 1846, Lord John Russell came to power at the head of the old Whig party. Two more factory acts established the long-awaited ten-hour day and the first public health act began a long process of improving urban life (Chapter 8). Russell tried (but failed) to bring about the religious equality in which he fervently believed. But the Whigs were no more prepared than were the Tories to take seriously the Chartists' demand for a more democratic system of government.

Thus ended the reforming endeavours of the early 19th century. Whether the 'Age of Reform' is an apt title for this 30-year period is for the student to decide (Chapter 10).

Chronology of the Age of Reform

1820	Death of George III and accession of George IV
	General election keeps Tories under Liverpool in power
1822	Peel becomes Home Secretary
1823	Reduction of some import duties
	Prison reforms
	Daniel O'Connell forms Catholic Association in Ireland
1824	Repeal of the Combination Acts
1825	Curbs placed on strikes and picketing
1826	General election confirms Tories in power

1827   February: Liverpool resigns and Canning succeeds him
           August: Canning dies and Goderich becomes Prime Minister
           Reforms in the criminal law

1828   Goderich resigns and Wellington becomes Prime Minister
           O'Connell wins by-election but cannot take his seat
           Repeal of the Test and Corporation Acts
           Revision of the Corn Laws (sliding scale)

1829   Roman Catholic Emancipation
           Metropolitan Police Force founded

1830   Death of George IV and accession of William IV
           June-August: General election gives indecisive result
           Agricultural riots
           November: resignation of Wellington
           Lord Grey forms Whig government

1831   March: First Reform bill introduced and defeated
           March-May: General election increases Whig majority
           September: Second Reform bill passed in Commons
           October-November: Riots in towns after defeat of Second
           Reform bill in Lords

1832   March: Third Reform bill passed in Commons
           May: Resignation of Grey after Lords insist on amendments
           Constitutional crisis and unrest in country
           June: Grey resumes office and Lords pass Reform bill
           after king threatens to create new peers
           December: General election with decisive Whig victory

1833   Abolition of slavery in British colonies
           Factory Act
           Grant to religious societies for building schools
           Irish Church bill
           Beginning of the Oxford Movement

1834   July: Grey resigns and Melbourne becomes Prime Minister
           Poor Law Amendment Act
           November: Melbourne resigns and Peel forms government
           Appointment of Ecclesiastical Commission
           Peel issues Tamworth Manifesto

1835   General election with some Tory gains
           April: Peel resigns and Melbourne resumes office
           Municipal Corporations Act
           Prison inspectorate established

1836   Ecclesiastical reforms
           Tithe Commutation Act
           Civil registration of births, marriages and deaths

1837   June: death of William IV and accession of Queen Victoria
           General election returns Whigs with reduced majority
           Beginning of trade depression

1838   People's Charter published
        Anti-Corn Law League founded
1839   Rejection of First Chartist petition in parliament
        May: Melbourne resigns but Queen's refusal to change Whig
        ladies of the bedchamber prevents Peel from taking office
        Melbourne resumes office
        Chartist rising in Newport
        Appointment of permanent Committee for Education
1840   Penny Post introduced
        Report of Import Duties Committee
1841   July: General election returns Conservative majority
        August: Melbourne resigns and Peel becomes Prime Minister
1842   Peel's budget reduces tariffs and restores income tax
        Second Chartist petition rejected in parliament
        Wave of strikes and riots
        Report on the Sanitary Condition of the Labouring Poor
        Mines Act
1844   Bank Charter Act and Companies Act
        Railways Act
        Factory Act
        Royal Commission on Health of Towns
1845   Peel's budget reduces more duties and retains income tax
        Maynooth grant leads to resignation of Gladstone
        Beginning of Irish potato famine
        Peel tries to resign but Whigs cannot form government
1846   Repeal of the Corn Laws
        June: Peel resigns and Russell forms Whig government
        Pupil-teacher scheme introduced
1847   General election confirms Whigs in power
        Factory Act
1848   Failure of Third Chartist petition
        Public Health Act
1849   Further reduction of import duties
        Repeal of the Navigation Acts
1850   Factory Act
        Death of Peel after riding accident

1 CHANGING TIMES

'Let the great world spin for ever down the ringing grooves of change.'
The poet, Alfred Tennyson, thought of this line as he rode in the first train
from Liverpool to Manchester in 1830. He was, of course, mistaken in
thinking that trains run in grooves, but he expressed an awareness of
rushing change which many people shared in the three decades covered
by this book. The main cause of the transformation was what we now call
the Industrial Revolution. In the late 18th and early 19th centuries new
methods and a greater output in the textile, iron and coal industries, as
well as in agriculture and transport, were making Britain the most
prosperous country in the world. Factories were being built to
accommodate newly invented machines. Towns were expanding to house
the industrial work-force. The population was growing fast and was
concentrated more in the coal- and iron-producing parts of the country.
Social relations were altering so radically that the new terms 'middle
class' and 'working class' were coined to describe them. Though most
modern historians would agree with F. M. L. Thompson that 'in 1830, the
day when typical English men and women would be town dwellers or
factory workers lay emphatically in the future', there is no doubt that life
was changing more rapidly than it had ever done before. [A–B]

Whether it was becoming better or worse is a question on which
contemporaries disagreed. Traditionalists and champions of the labouring
classes lamented the passing of happier days, while progressives and
entrepreneurs hailed the improvements industrialisation had wrought.
Today there is still no agreement. Some historians (known as 'optimists')
use wage and price figures to prove that all classes of people were better off
in the early 19th century. 'Pessimistic' historians do not dispute that there
was greater general prosperity, but they emphasise the extreme
fluctuations in real wages [money wages compared with prices] and the
many exceptions to the rule, like the handloom weavers; they also say
that, for the majority, the living and working environment deteriorated.
[C–H and Chapters 7 and 8]

Difficult though it is to generalise on this matter, there is no doubt that
industrialisation caused new problems as well as bringing unprecedented
prosperity. Increasingly, in the years following the Napoleonic wars,
writers, reformers and pressure groups drew attention to evils like the
crippling of children in factories, the deterioration in family life, the
overcrowding of workers in unhealthy cities and the sharpening of class
conflict. The most vivid descriptions came from novelists, poets and
essayists – though they did not usually propose solutions. [I–K]

The more practical reformers were divided into two groups, both of which challenged the prevailing *laissez-faire* belief that society and the economy would flourish if only governments left them alone. On the one hand, followers of Jeremy Bentham (known as Benthamites) employed the 'Utilitarian' principle to justify limited state intervention: they insisted that reform must be useful, must promote the greatest happiness of the greatest number of people. On the other hand, humanitarians (or philanthropists), inspired often by strong religious belief, urged governments to protect poor and defenceless sections of the community from gross exploitation. Supporters of these differing views were to be found in both political parties. But Whigs were more often influenced by Benthamism while humanitarians tended to be Tory. Radicals derided both schools of thought and called for far-reaching change. [L–O]

Throughout the period, too, many associations developed to represent particular classes and interests. These pressure groups called for measures which would redress their own grievances. Their aims and methods will be illustrated in succeeding chapters, as will the laws which reluctant governments passed in response to moral and even physical force. Fear was, perhaps, the strongest motive for reform. Ever since the collapse of the old order in France politicians had been haunted by a vision of the breakdown of society in Britain. [P]

A Percentage of the population of England and Wales living in towns

	Towns 2,500–10,000	Towns 10,000–100,000	Towns over 100,000	All towns
1750	5	2	11	18
1801	6	6	11	23
1851	10	13	11	34
1901	10	19	25	54

from *Cambridge Social History of Britain* ed. F. M. L. Thompson (1990)

B George Eliot (the pen-name of Mary Ann Evans) demonstrates her awareness of social change in this passage from her novel *Felix Holt*, set in the Midlands in the 1830s

Treby Magna, on which the Reform Bill thrust the new honour of being a polling-place, had been, at the beginning of the century, quite a typical old market-town, lying in pleasant sleepiness among green pastures, with a rush-fringed river meandering through them. Its principal street had various handsome and tall-windowed brick houses with walled gardens behind them; and, at the end, where it widened into the market-place, there was the cheerful rough-stuccoed front of that excellent inn, The Marquis of Granby, where the farmers put up their gigs, not only on fair and market days, but also on exceptional Sundays when they came to church. And the church was one of those fine old English structures . . . standing in a broad churchyard with a line of solemn yew-trees beside it, and lifting a majestic tower and spire far above the red-and-purple roofs of the town . . . Such was the old-fashioned, grazing, brewing, wool-packing, cheese-loading life of Treby Magna, until there befell new conditions, complicating its relating with the rest of the world, and awakening in it that higher consciousness which is known to bring higher pains. First came the canal; next, the working of the coal-mines at Spoxton, two miles off the town, and, . . . at last . . . a tape manufactory.

In this way it happened that Treby Magna gradually passed from being simply a respectable market-town – the heart of a great rural district, where the only trade was with the local landed interest – and took on the more complex life brought by mines and manufactures, which belong more to the great circulating system of the nation than to the local system.

from *Felix Holt, the Radical* by George Eliot (1866)

C The reformer and doctor, J. P. Kay (who later became Sir James Kay-Shuttleworth), describes conditions in Manchester

The population . . . is crowded into one dense mass, in cottages separated by narrow, unpaved, and almost pestilential streets, in an atmosphere loaded with the smoke and exhalations of a large manufacturing city. The operatives [machine workers] are congregated in rooms and workshops during twelve hours in a day, in an enervating, heated atmosphere, which is frequently loaded with dust or filaments of cotton, or impure from constant respiration, or from other causes. They are engaged in an employment which absorbs their attention, and unremittingly employs their physical energies. They are drudges who watch the movements, and assist the operations, of a mighty material force, which toils with an energy ever unconscious of fatigue. The persevering labour of the operative must rival the mathematical precision, the incessant motion, the exhaustless power of the machine.

from *The Moral and Physical Condition of the Working-Classes* by J. P. Kay (1832)

D A retired military man records his very different impressions of Leeds

There can be no spectacle more grateful to the heart of an Englishman than, viewing the interior of a manufactory of machinery, to observe the features of each hard-working mechanic blackened by smoke, yet radiant with the light of intelligence, – to contrast with his humble station the lines of fervid thought that mark his countenance and direct his sinewy arm, and to reflect that to such a combination of the powers of mind and body England owes her present state of commercial greatness. It is no less pleasing to consider, that although particular classes of men have suffered by the substitution of machinery for manual labour, such evils arise from the the mutability [changeable nature] of human affairs, – are such as the most zealous philanthropist cannot avert; and, lastly, of themselves insignificant compared with the general demand for labour throughout the country.

from *A Home Tour through the Manufacturing Districts of England* by Sir George Head (1835)

E A modern economic historian states the optimistic view
Since average *per capita* [per head] income increased, since there was no trend in distribution against the workers, since (after 1815) prices fell while money wages remained constant, since *per capita* consumption of food and other consumer goods increased, and since government increasingly intervened in economic life to protect or raise living standards, then the real wages of the majority of English workers were rising in the years 1800 to 1850 . . . Economy and society were in the process of rapid change, and the opportunities for wealth and social advancement were greater than they had ever been before.

from an article by R. M. Hartwell (1961)

F The Marxist historian Eric Hobsbawm argues the pessimistic case; he says there is 'no excuse' for Hartwell's ignoring the quality of life
Not to admit [the social stresses of industrialisation] is to make any understanding impossible. As is often the case, the poets saw things which the vulgar economists did not . . . Charles Dickens, whose criticism of Coketown [the imaginary industrial town in his novel *Hard Times*] was not merely that its inhabitants were poor and economically insecure, but that it was inhuman, expressed the anguish of a generation more profoundly than those who might merely have observed, with justice, that its drains were defective and something ought to be done about it. The historian forgets at his peril that the problem of the social impact of the industrial revolution is not whether men live by white bread or brown bread, no meat or roast beef; even though it can be shown that in our period it did not actually give them any extra roast beef. It is also, that men do not live by bread alone.

from an article by E. Hobsbawm (1963)

G Twenty years later economic historians use a graph to demonstrate a rise in real wages for adult males in full-time work

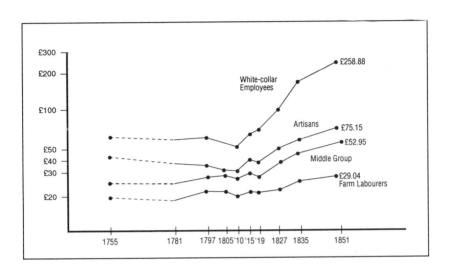

H But other historians still suggest that this is an over-simple view
Our evidence supports the view that fairly substantial gains in material standards were achieved over the course of industrialisation by the British working class. But . . . earnings and income growth were far from continuous, and the severity of interruptions and setbacks in material progress has been underestimated by analyses based on trends in relatively static wage rates . . . For the period as a whole family incomes grew less than did male earnings, so welfare gains deduced from the latter may overstate actual improvements. Investigation of family incomes has also revealed that industrialization brought with it greater inequality among families than has been previously assumed.

from an article by S. Horrell and J. Humphries (1992)

I Many 'social novels' were written, like Dickens's *Hard Times*, to convey the hardship caused by the trade slump of the early 1840s. One such novel is *Mary Barton* by Mrs Gaskell, the wife of a minister in Manchester. In this extract the author explains the bitterness which led Mary's father, John Barton, to become a trade union leader and a Chartist
He was a good, steady workman, and, as such, pretty certain of steady employment. But he spent all he got with the confidence (you may also call it improvidence) of one who was willing, and believed himself able, to supply all his wants by his own exertions. And when his master

suddenly failed, and all hands in that mill were turned back, one Tuesday morning, with the news that Mr Hunter had stopped, Barton had only a few shillings to rely on; but he had good heart of being employed at some other mill, and accordingly, before returning home, he spent some hours in going from factory to factory, asking for work. But at every mill was some sign of depression of trade; some were working short hours, some were turning off hands, and for weeks Barton was out of work, living on credit. It was during this time his little son, the apple of his eye . . . fell ill of the scarlet fever. They dragged him through the crisis, but his life hung on a gossamer thread. Everything, the doctor said, depended on good nourishment . . . to keep up the little boy's strength . . . Mocking words! when the commonest food in the house would not furnish one little meal . . . Hungry himself, almost to an animal pitch of ravenousness, but with the bodily pain swallowed up in anxiety for his little sinking lad, Barton stood at one of the shop windows where all edible luxuries are displayed; haunches of venison, Stilton cheeses, moulds of jelly – all appetising sights to the common passer by. And out of this shop came Mrs Hunter! She crossed to her carriage, followed by the shopman loaded with purchases for a party. The door was quickly slammed to, and she drove away; and Barton returned home with a bitter spirit of wrath in his heart, to see his only boy a corpse!

from *Mary Barton* by Elizabeth Gaskell (1848)

J Another novel which sought to reveal social injustice was *Sybil* by the future Prime Minister, Benjamin Disraeli. Here he describes the thoughts of a handloom weaver as he sits down to his twelve hours of labour at the rate of a penny an hour

Why am I here? Why am I, and six hundred thousand subjects of the Queen, honest, loyal, and industrious, why are we, after manfully struggling for years, and each year sinking lower in the scale, why are we driven from our innocent happy homes, our country cottages that we loved, first to bide in close towns without comforts, and gradually to crouch into cellars . . . first the ordinary conveniences of life, then raiment, and, at length, food, vanishing from us? It is that the capitalist has found a slave that has supplanted the labour and ingenuity of man. Once he was an artisan: at the best, he now only watches machines; and even that occupation slips from his grasp, to the woman and the child. The capitalist flourishes, he amasses immense wealth; we sink lower and lower . . . And yet they tell us that the interests of Capital and Labour are identical.

from *Sybil or the Two Nations* by B. Disraeli (1845)

K The influential writer, Thomas Carlyle, criticises the new social order with a bitterly ironic comparison

The master of horses, when the summer labour is done, has to feed his horses through the winter. If he said to his horses: 'Quadrupeds, I have no longer work for you; but work exists abundantly over the world: are you ignorant (or must I read you Political-Economy lectures) that the steam-engine always in the long-run creates additional work? Railways are forming in one quarter of this earth, canals in another, much cartage is wanted; somewhere in Europe, Asia, Africa or America, doubt it not, ye will find cartage: go and seek cartage, and good go with you!' They, with protrusive upper lip, snort dubious; signifying that Europe, Asia, Africa and America lie somewhat out of their beat; that what cartage may be wanted there is not too well known to them. They can find no cartage. They gallop distracted along highways, all fenced in to the right and to the left: finally, under pains of hunger, they take to leaping fences; eating foreign property, and – we know the rest. Ah, it is not a joyful mirth, it is sadder than tears, the laugh Humanity is forced to, at Laissez-faire applied to the poor peasants, in a world like our Europe of the year 1839!

from *Chartism* by T. Carlyle (1839)

L A classic statement of the *laissez-faire* theory

It cannot be denied that there is more busy, prying, laborious benevolence in England than there is in any country under the sun . . . Instead of any longer contenting ourselves and soothing our consciences with idly nibbling at the outskirts of a vast and growing mischief in our social state, – let us have the courage and candour to go at once to the origin of the evil – to strike at the source of that malady which has so long withered up the physical energies and moral virtues of our people. Let us unfetter the springs of the national industry, in the full confidence that, if we do so, it has an expansive elasticity within it, sufficient to absorb into profitable employment all those numbers whom it is now the fashion to consider as redundant . . . Under a system of unrestricted freedom, the field of employment is capable of this indefinite enlargement.

from an article in *Edinburgh Review* (1844)

M Philosopher John Stuart Mill gives an example of how government intervention can be justified on the utilitarian principle

Education . . . is one of those things which it is admissable in principle that a government should provide for the people. The case is one to which the reasons of the non-interference principle do not necessarily or universally extend . . . There are certain primary elements and means of knowledge that all human beings born into the community should acquire during childhood. If their parents . . . have the power of obtaining for them this instruction, and fail to do it, they commit a double breach of duty, towards the children themselves and towards the members of the community generally, who are all liable to suffer seriously from the consequences of ignorance and want of education in their fellow-citizens. It is therefore an allowable exercise of the powers of government to impose on parents the legal obligation of giving elementary instruction to children. This, however, cannot fairly be done, without taking measures to insure that such instruction shall be always accessible to them, either gratuitously or at a trifling expense.

from *Principles of Political Economy* by J. S. Mill (1848)

N The Tory reformer Lord Shaftesbury urges a humanitarian approach towards children working in factories

Can it be pronounced necessary to our social welfare, or national prosperity, that children of the tenderest years should toil, amid every discomfort and agony of posture, and foul atmosphere, for fifteen or sixteen successive hours? . . . Can it be for our honour or our safety, that their young hearts, instead of being trained in the ways of temperance and virtue, should be acquiring knowledge of those vices which they will afterwards practise as adults? . . . Let your laws, we say to Parliament, assume the proper functions of law, protect those for whom neither wealth, nor station, nor age has raised a bulwark [defence] against tyranny; . . . [this] will give content instead of bitterness, engraft obedience on rebellion, raise purity from corruption, and 'life from the dead' – but there is no time to be lost.

from *Infant Labour* in *Quarterly Review* (1840)

O Agricultural labourers express their anger during the 'Swing' riots of 1830

Sir

We beg to say that if the sentences of the men in kent & all others for rioting is not reduseed to 3 months & all those taken heairafter to 1 monts ditto all the woods to a hedge stick on the duke of rishmans estaite with that of the other ministere the crown lands magestrates constabels & all engaged in takeing & triing the said men shall be all burnt up even to a furse bush but we promis faithfully if you comply with our request we will refrain from it. What we want is Work and fair wages dont think that the reward will induse our men to split we have all put our hand to the match and we cannot betray each other and are determined to carry on and to set our starveing Countramen at liberty. There is only 2 things to be done then we shall have peace & plenty that is machinery put down and the clergy paid out of the publick revenue and an income tax put on to take the abuse of the farmer in lieu of the tithes.

from a letter sent to the Duke of Richmond in December 1830

P A Whig politician proposes an inquiry into the alarming state of the nation in 1830

The present situation of things in this country was the most alarming, he would say, that had ever been witnessed in any period of our history. He would not except times that had passed by, and which he himself was old enough in some degree to remember – not even the period of the French Revolution . . . The state of the country was more perilous at present than it had been then or at any former period . . . The great majority of the industrious classes . . . were afflicted with intolerable distress, which naturally exciting general discontent, might unhappily hereafter, should no means be adopted to remove the cause of it, break out into general disaffection.

from a speech by Lord Stanhope in the House of Lords, 25 February 1830

Questions

1 Compare the reliability of sources A–D for judging the nature of social change in the first half of the 19th century. **(8 marks)**

2 What types of evidence do you think the historians in sources E–H have used to reach their conclusions on workers' standard of living? Explain whether you find the optimistic or the pessimistic view more convincing. **(8 marks)**

3 Examine the methods used by the writers of sources I–K to convey social injustice. **(8 marks)**

4 Discuss the attitudes to government intervention shown in sources L–N. **(8 marks)**

5 To what extent does source O justify the fears expressed in source P? **(8 marks)**

2 ALTERING THE CONSTITUTION

In October 1831 the Whig Lord Chancellor, Henry Brougham, fell to his knees in the House of Lords as he concluded a long speech in support of the Parliamentary Reform Bill with the words: 'I warn you – I implore you – yea, on my bended knees, I supplicate you – Reject not this Bill.' He then found that he could not get up again and noble lords had to lift him back on to the woolsack. Such dramatic behaviour in the normally staid upper house suggests that this was a question of extreme importance. Why did the Reform Bill matter so much?

The main reason is that the old system of representation was quite unsuited to the changing times. Many ancient boroughs, all sending two members to parliament, had decayed: these were known as 'rotten' or 'pocket' boroughs because they had so few voters and these were controlled by the local landowners. On the other hand, many growing industrial towns were not separate parliamentary constituencies. The voting qualification in the boroughs was sometimes wide, as in 'potwalloper' boroughs where any man owning a fireplace on which he could boil a pot was entitled to be an elector. More often the qualification was narrow, being confined, for instance, to members of the town corporation. Each county, whether sparsely or densely populated, was also represented by two MPs. There the franchise depended on a man's possessing a freehold worth 40 shillings a year. As the ballot was not conducted in secret, voters could be influenced or bribed. What all this amounted to was that the aristocracy and landed gentry controlled elections while the middle classes (who now played such an important part in the economy) did not usually have the right to vote, much less exert any political influence. The working class was almost entirely excluded from the parliamentary system – though conservatives claimed that, in some mysterious way, an aristocratic parliament represented the whole community. [A–D]

Since the 1780s there had been much criticism of the 'Old Corruption' (as the reformer, William Cobbett, called it). This criticism had reached a peak in the years immediately after the Napoleonic wars but had died down during the 1820s. By 1830 breaches made in the 'unalterable constitution', notably by Roman Catholic Emancipation [Chapter 3], combined with further economic distress to cause acute pressure for parliamentary reform. In major towns Political Unions of the Middle and Working Classes were formed – though their union was more in name than in reality. When the Whigs took office after the fall of Wellington they quickly prepared a Parliamentary Reform Bill, which Lord John

Russell introduced in March 1831. It was comprehensive enough to make MPs gasp. Parliamentary seats were to be redistributed from sparsely inhabited boroughs to large towns and more populous counties. The new franchise was carefully calculated to include most middle-class, though very few working-class, men. Convinced as they were of the wise moderation of their bill, Lord Grey and his ministers did not realise how difficult it would be to get through parliament. It scraped through the second reading, supported, ironically, by some ultra-Tories who reckoned that a representative House of Commons would never have allowed Roman Catholic Emancipation. But it was rejected at the committee stage. A second 'reform' election secured the Whigs a greatly increased majority and the Commons duly passed a slightly amended bill in September 1831. Despite Brougham's eloquent plea, however, the House of Lords was more convinced by Lord Eldon's prediction that it would be fatal to sacrifice 'one atom of our glorious Constitution'; the peers rejected it by 41 votes in October. [E–H]

By this time there was so much excitement over the bill that many were convinced (as was the government) that the consequence of its defeat would be revolution. Inflammatory language was used at mass meetings and in the radical press. During the autumn of 1831 there were also serious riots in several cities. The greatest disturbances occurred in Bristol, where public buildings (including the Bishop's Palace and the prisons) were attacked; as troops restored order after several days of rioting 12 people were killed, 94 wounded and 102 arrested. Fear of further trouble strengthened the determination of the Whigs. A third bill was introduced and passed through the Commons, only to fail at the committee stage in the Lords. The Whigs' sole recourse was to persuade the king to create enough new peers to allow the bill to pass. When William IV refused to do this, in May 1832, Grey resigned. For a week the Duke of Wellington struggled to form a government – against the background of a furious campaign in favour of 'The Bill, the whole Bill and nothing but the Bill'. He was unable to do so because Peel steadfastly refused to countenance any measure of parliamentary reform. The Whigs pressed on and the king became compliant. Bowing to the threat that their house would be swamped with new peers, the Lords passed the Bill in June.

It is impossible to know whether the predicted revolution would have occurred if the Bill had failed. Most historians argue that Radicals like Francis Place and James Mill relied on a policy of bluff to terrify the upper classes and that the authorities had no real difficulty in maintaining control. Some also suggest that, although a successful rising was not feasible in 1832, it might well have happened when hard times returned during the 1840s. It is generally agreed, though, that public opinion played a vital role in the passing of the bill. [I–M]

The 'Great Reform Act' was unquestionably an important issue in its day. Opinions were then, and are now, divided on its results. It did not bring about the disasters dreaded by conservatives nor the harmony hoped for by liberals. In fact Grey had not intended the destruction of the old system but its preservation; so it is not difficult for historians to show that pocket boroughs survived, as did uncontested or corrupt elections and under-representation in parts of the country. Although the electorate had increased by 50 per cent, still only 1 in 7 of Britain's adult male population were entitled to vote. There had never been any question of the working classes being given the franchise, though many who had supported the bill did not fully realise that until after it had been passed. From their sense of betrayal the Chartist movement developed in the late 1830s. Women supporters of the reform movement (some of whom are shown in K) had never been under any such illusion; in fact they had usually come to meetings wearing white to symbolise their selflessness (as well as their virtue). [N–Q]

These shortcomings of the 'Great Reform Act' are very apparent. It was, nevertheless, very important both as a step towards greater democracy and in its immediate consequences. Politicians now had to work harder to win votes. This meant both that parties became more organised in rounding up electors and that candidates had to express concern on a wider range of social issues. The greater or lesser results of this concern were manifested in the 'age of reform'.

A The Duke of Wellington defends the old system and brings about his own resignation

He was fully convinced that the country possessed at the present moment a legislature which answered all the good purposes of legislation, and this to a greater degree than any legislature ever had answered in any country whatever. He would go further and say, that the legislature and the system of representation possessed the full and entire confidence of the country – deservedly possessed that confidence – and the discussions of the legislature had a very great influence over the opinions of the country . . . The representation of the people at present contained a large body of the property of the country, in which the landed interests had a preponderating influence.

from a speech in the House of Lords, 2 November 1830

B Lord John Russell conducts MPs on a guided tour of the unreformed constituencies

Allow me to imagine, for a moment, a stranger from some distant country, who should arrive in England to examine our institutions . . . He would have been told, that the proudest boast of this celebrated country was its political freedom . . . What then would be his surprise, if he were taken by this guide, whom he had asked to conduct him to one of the places of election, to a green mound and told, that this green mound sent two members to Parliament – or, to be taken to a stone wall, with three niches in it, and to be told these three niches sent two Members to Parliament – or, if he were shown a green park, with many signs of flourishing vegetable life, but none of human habitation, and told that this green park sent two Members to Parliament? But his surprise would increase to astonishment if he were carried into the North of England, where he would see large flourishing towns, full of trade and activity, containing vast magazines of wealth and manufactures, and were told that these places had no Representatives in the Assembly which was said to represent the people . . . His surprise would be turned into disgust at the gross venality and corruption which he would find to pervade the electors.

from a speech in the House of Commons, 1 March 1831

C William Thackeray pokes fun at the haphazard and privileged nature of the old parliamentary system in his novel *Vanity Fair*

Among the most respected of the names beginning in C, which the Court Guide contained in the year 18--, was that of Crawley, Sir Pitt, Baronet, Great Gaunt Street, and Queen's Crawley, Hants. This honourable name had figured constantly also in the Parliamentary list for many years, in conjunction with that of a number of other worthy gentlemen who sat in turns for the borough. It is related, with regard to the borough of Queen's Crawley, that Queen Elizabeth in one of her progresses, stopping at Crawley to breakfast, was so delighted with some remarkably fine Hampshire beer which was then presented to her by the Crawley of the day (a handsome gentleman with a trim beard and a good leg), that she forthwith erected Crawley into a borough to send two members to Parliament; and the place, from the day of that illustrious visit, took the name of Queen's Crawley, which it holds up to the present moment. And though, by the lapse of time, and those mutations which age produces in empires, cities and boroughs, Queen's Crawley was no longer so populous a place as it had been in Queen Bess's time – nay, was come down to that condition of borough which used to be denominated rotten – yet, as Sir Pitt Crawley would say with perfect justice in his elegant way, 'Rotten! be hanged – it produces me a good fifteen hundred a year.'

from *Vanity Fair* by W. M. Thackeray (1847)

D One of the most influential agitators for reform, both in the post-war period and in 1830–2, was the journalist William Cobbett. In this passage from *Rural Rides* he describes (in his usual emphatic style) a rotten borough in Wiltshire

The labourers along here seem very poor indeed . . . I never saw *country* people . . . so miserable as these. There were some very pretty girls, but ragged as colts and pale as ashes. The day was cold too, and frost hardly from the ground; and their blue arms and lips would have made any heart ache but that of a seat-seller or a loan-jobber. A little after passing by these poor things, whom I left, cursing, as I went, those who had brought them to this state, I came to a group of shabby houses upon a hill. While the boy was watering the horses, I asked the ostler the name of the place; and, as the old women say, 'you might have knocked me down with a feather,' when he said, '*Great Bedwin*'. The whole of the houses are not intrinsically worth a thousand pounds. There stood a thing out in the middle of the place, about 25 feet long and 15 wide, being a room stuck up on unhewed stone pillars about 10 feet high. It was the Town Hall, where the ceremony of returning the *two Members* is performed. 'This place sends Members to Parliament, don't it?' said I to the ostler. 'Yes, Sir.' 'Who are the Members now?' 'I *don't know*, indeed, Sir.'

from *Rural Rides* by W. Cobbett (1853 edn.)

E Thomas Macaulay, who was a Whig MP as well as a historian, makes one of several eloquent speeches in defence of a moderate extension of the suffrage
If the labourers of England were in that state in which I, from my soul, wish to see them, – if employment were always plentiful, wages always high, food always cheap, – if a large family were considered not as an encumbrance, but as a blessing – the principal objectives to Universal Suffrage [votes for everyone] would, I think, be removed . . . But, unhappily, the lower orders in England, as in all old countries, are occasionally in a state of great distress . . . [which] makes even wise men irritable, unreasonable, and credulous – eager for immediate relief – heedless of remote consequences . . . It blunts their judgement, it inflames their passions, it makes them prone to believe those who flatter them, and to distrust those who serve them . . . I oppose Universal Suffrage because I think that it would produce a destructive revolution. I support this measure, because I am sure that it is our best security against a revolution . . . All history is full of revolutions, produced by causes similar to those which are operating in England. A portion of the community which had been of no account, expands and becomes strong. It demands a place in the system, suited, not to its former weakness but to its present power . . . If this is refused, then comes the struggle between the young energy of one class, and the ancient privileges of another . . . Such is the struggle which the middle classes in England are maintaining against an ancient aristocracy.

from a speech in the House of Commons, 2 March 1831

F Peel argues that the working classes are better served by the existing parliament than by the proposed system of representation which would exclude them

It is an immense advantage that there is at present no class of people, however humble, which is not entitled to a voice in the election of representatives . . . The individual is limited, and properly limited, within narrow bounds; but the class is represented. It has its champion within your walls, the organ of its feeling, and the guardian of its interests. But what will be the effect of cutting off altogether the communication between this House and all that class of society which is above pauperism, and below the arbitrary line of £10 rental which you have selected?

from a speech in the House of Commons, 3 March 1831

G The *Poor Man's Guardian*, a widely read working-class newspaper established in 1831, opposed the Reform Bill from the beginning

Need we now repeat the opinion which from the very first moment we formed of this delusive and dangerous measure, and which deep consideration and all the fulsome and party reasoning brought forward in support of it have only tended to confirm? Yes, friends and fellow-countrymen, we protest that this measure is a mere *trick* to strengthen against your rightful claims the tottering exclusiveness of our 'blessed constitution.' It is clear, *we* GAIN nothing by it; but it is said, that these middle men, whom this measure admits into a share of the legislature, will be more inclined to hear our appeal for justice, and will return a majority favourable to it: think it not; – why, already – before even they have gained their own admittance – do they not shut the doors of Parliament against you?

from *Poor Man's Guardian*, 15 October 1831

H The Prime Minister, Lord Grey, warns the Lords of what will happen if they reject the Bill

Will your Lordships reject a measure sanctioned by an overwhelming and irresistible majority of the Representatives of the people in the other House – the people themselves, at the same time, roused and agitated from one end of the country to the other, crowding earnestly to the bar of your House [where petitions are presented] and claiming a restitution of their rights? . . . I cannot conceal from your Lordships my apprehension that the result of its rejection will be most dangerous to the best interests of the country . . . I implore your Lordships to consider what will be the consequences of the rejection of this measure; and whether, if rejected now, it can be finally put aside. May you, my Lords be wise in time . . . and avoid those dangers which will inevitably arise from your rejection of this measure, and secure, by its adoption, peace and conciliation in the country.

from a speech in the House of Lords, 3 October 1831

I A clergyman is horrified by the riots in Bristol
In the afternoon we heard that the multitude was assembled in much greater masses, and about four o'clock we saw the new City and County Gaol in flames; afterwards the Bridewell and another prison in the Gloucester Road, about a mile from Bristol. In the course of the evening Queen's Square was fired and the Bishop's palace. Of Queen's Square two whole sides have been burnt down, including the Mansion House and . . . the Custom House. The cathedral was preserved, and is still standing, but was attempted. Other property to an immense amount is also destroyed. This morning an actual slaughter has taken place; it is supposed, though of course nothing precise can be known at present, that above seventy persons have been killed, besides a large number who have been wounded. The military charged through some of the principal streets, cutting right and left. What will be the event of this evening and night I know not, but I believe that the events of yesterday will never be effaced from the recollection of my family . . . May God preserve us and our guilty land! Our wretched Ministers have raised a storm which, I fear, it will not be in their power to direct or control.

from a letter by the Revd. J. L. Jackson, 31 October 1831

J Working-class leaders express different reasons for abhorring such violence
Unfortunately . . . our poor deluded brethren have been sadly rioting. Nottingham Castle (the Duke of Newcastle's) has been destroyed by fire, and elsewhere great damage done to *Tory* property. We cannot but say that the destruction of their property is but a just judgement upon those who make it such *an exclusive qualification* but we like not to see what so much labour has produced, so wantonly destroyed, independently of the danger to which the destroyers of it expose themselves; – think you that these *Whigs*, although you risk your lives to forward *their own* delusive and treacherous designs, will not order out their blood-liveried assassins to murder you if you 'tumultuously assemble together', to the danger of their sacred rights of property? . . . We entreat you – not on account of the danger – but on account of morality, to restrain all acts of violence against your tyrants, nor in any way warrant their cruel scorn, their contemptuous reviling; – do not gratify them by being 'the mob' they imagine and wish you to be.

from *Poor Man's Guardian*, 22 October 1831

K A contemporary print shows a large gathering of Political Unions on New Hall Hill, Birmingham in May 1832

L A Whig MP reports Francis Place's view of events in May 1832
19 May
I went to Place. He told me that there would positively have been a
rising if Wellington had recovered power yesterday. Everything was
arranged for it; he himself would not have slept at home.

from *Recollections of a Long Life* by J. C. Hobhouse (1865)

M A modern historian gives a balanced view of events
In assessing Grey's policy it is . . . essential to recognise that his primary
objective was to prevent a revolution. I have expressed doubt of the
chances of a successful rising in 1832. But this is not to say that the old
system could have gone on much longer. If it is legitimate to postulate
the same economic developments without the political changes, one
can hardly see the old regime surviving the acute recessions of the
1840s. Even William IV, more inclined to Toryism than Whiggism,
agreed that some reform was inescapable.

from *Parliamentary Reform 1640–1832* by J.Cannon (1972)

**N As part of the celebrations in 1832 this Hymn was written for the
Rotheram Political Union by a poet already well-known for his
attacks on the Corn Laws**
We thank Thee, Lord of earth and heav'n,
For hope, and strength, and triumph given!
We thank Thee that the fight is won,
Although our work is but begun.

We met, we crush'd the evil powers;
A nobler task must now be ours –
Their victims maim'd and poor to feed,
And bind the bruised and broken reed.

Oh, let not Ruin's will be done,
When Freedom's fight is fought and won!
The deed of Brougham, Russell, Grey,
Outlives the night! Lord give us day!

from a poem by Ebenezer Elliott

O Anglican Churchman, Hurrell Froude, regrets the passing of old ways
'Tis sad to watch Time's desolating hand
    Doom noblest things to premature decay:
    The Feudal Court, the Patriarchal sway
Of kings, the cheerful homage of a land
Unskill'd in treason, every social band

That taught to rule with sweetness, and obey
With dignity, swept one by one away.

from *Farewell to Toryism* by H. Froude (1833)

P Thackeray's character, Sir Pitt Crawley (son of the old baronet) finds that he has lost his influence at Queen's Crawley
... where, after the passing of the Reform Bill, Sir Pitt and his family constantly resided now. All idea of a Peerage was now out of the question, the Baronet's two seats in Parliament being lost. He was both out of pocket and out of spirits by that catastrophe, failed in his health, and prophesied the speedy ruin of the Empire.

from *Vanity Fair* by W. M. Thackeray (1847)

Q But William Cobbett looks forward to further changes
When the hungry and angry half-starved labourers complain of their sufferings, and are ready to break into acts of violence, will they be quieted by telling them, that they must not complain *now* for that they have got *reform*; will they, at the sound of that word, cease to harbour vindictive thoughts relative to those they deem their oppressors? Oh, no! the reform must be something more than a *bill*, something more than a bit of printed paper; it must, to be productive of harmony, cause something to be done to better the state of the people; and, in order to do this, it must produce, and quickly too, not only a change in the management of the affairs of the country, but *a very great change*.

from a lecture given at Manchester, 26 December 1831.

Questions

1 Use sources A–D to construct arguments which could have been used in the early 19th century a) to defend and b) to attack the existence of rotten boroughs. **(8 marks)**

2 Show how the new class-consciousness is revealed in sources E–G. **(8 marks)**

3 How useful are sources H–L in helping you to decide how close Britain was to revolution in 1831–2? **(10 marks)**

4 What further evidence do you think the historian in source M has used to reach his conclusion? **(6 marks)**

5 Compare the emotions with which the writers of sources N–Q greet the passing of the Reform Act. **(8 marks)**

3 SAVING THE CHURCH

Religious issues were strongly contested in the election which followed the 1832 Reform Act. Most Whig candidates promised in their speeches that the Anglican Church, like the British Constitution, should now be reformed. This gained widespread approval. But many churchmen shared the fears of the Revd Thomas Arnold, who lamented: 'The Church, as it now stands, no human power can save.'

The Anglican Church had become established after Henry VIII's break from Rome. Its Protestant beliefs were set out in the Book of Common Prayer and the Thirty-Nine Articles, unaltered since Elizabeth I's reign. The Act of Settlement of 1701 ensured that the monarch must always be a member of it. In the early 19th century the Church of England still wielded much political power, not only through the sovereign but also through its bishops who sat in the House of Lords. Its dominance was further ensured by the virtual monopoly its members enjoyed of the House of Commons, local corporations, the armed forces, the universities and the public schools. Its considerable wealth was derived both from its ownership of land and from its right to levy on all landowners living in its parishes the church rate and the tithe [a tenth of their income]. [A]

Criticism of this historic, privileged body came to a head in 1831–2, when the bishops in the House of Lords opposed the Reform Bill. Several were physically attacked and popular orators poured abuse on the Church. Pamphlets and newspapers condemned its wealth, the opulence of its bishops and the poverty of its curates, the non-residence and pluralism [holding of more than one post] of many clergymen and the shortage of churches in industrial towns. Most of this criticism was fair and many Tories and Churchmen agreed with Whig politicians that some reform was essential if the Established Church was to survive. [B]

Another reason for religion having become such an important political issue was the growth of Dissenting or Nonconformist sects outside the Church of England. The largest of these was Methodism, started by John Wesley in the 18th century as a movement within the Church of England but now a fast expanding independent denomination. There was also rapid growth in older Dissenting groups like Quakers, Baptists, Congregationalists and Presbyterians. Men and women (especially the latter) from the middle and more prosperous working classes were attracted to these more informal, spontaneous and enthusiastic forms of worship, in some of which women could play a more prominent role than was allowed in the Church of England. Like the growing Low Church element within the Church of England, all these sects were Evangelical. In other words, they emphasised salvation by faith, preaching the Gospel, Bible-reading and good works. [C–E]

By the 1830s, Dissenters were numerous enough to protest against the political and social dominance of the Anglicans and to claim equal rights. The liberal-Tory government had acceded to their demands in 1828 by repealing the Test and Corporation Acts which had officially (but not necessarily in practice) debarred them from civil office. A stream of pamphlets drew parliament's attention to Dissenters' remaining grievances: they still could not be legally married or conduct burial services in their own chapels; they could not take degrees at English universities; and they had to pay tithes and rates to the Anglican Church. [F–G]

Roman Catholics had even more to complain about. The growing number of those living in England was subject to the same disabilities as Protestant Dissenters. They also faced widespread prejudice and certain restrictions on the practice of their faith. But in Ireland, where Catholics constituted over 90 per cent of the population, the dominance of the Protestant Church of Ireland (which had been the Established Church in Ireland since the Act of Union in 1800) was flagrantly unjust. Daniel O'Connell's Catholic Association had forced the Tories to pass the Roman Catholic Emancipation Act in 1829; English and Irish Catholics could now become MPs and hold most government posts (even in theory that of Prime Minister) as long as they swore not to 'disturb or weaken the Protestant religion'. But Irish Catholics still had to pay tithes and church rates to support 22 bishops and 2,500 parishes of a Church to which only 7 per cent of the population belonged. Thus in the early 1830s Irish peasants began a campaign for the non-payment of tithes. [H–I]

Convinced that reform of the Church in Ireland was its most urgent task, the Whigs introduced the Irish Church Temporalities Bill in 1833. This suppressed ten bishoprics, abolished the church rate and suspended parishes where there were no Anglican worshippers. An additional clause proposed that the money saved might be used for educational or social (rather than for religious) purposes. This proposed 'burglary' raised such a storm of protest among Anglicans that it had to be dropped. The bill was passed but the dispute helped to force the Whigs out of office in 1834.

Peel was in power long enough to demonstrate the Tory Party's willingness to reform the Church. He appointed an Ecclesiastical Commission, consisting of government and church leaders, to work out the details of reform. When the Whigs returned to office in 1835 they enacted the Commission's cautious recommendations. In three acts they made bishops' stipends more equal, cut down pluralism and placed a limit on the number of appointments attached to cathedrals. The surplus money was used to supplement the incomes of poor clergy and to build new urban churches. [K]

With more controversial religious matters the increasingly weak Whig

29

government had less success. The Home Secretary, Lord John Russell, was anxious to render justice to the Irish but he could do no more than make minor changes in the payment of tithes. English Dissenters gained more rights: by the end of the 1830s they could marry in their own chapels, pay tithes at a more acceptable level, and take degrees at London University.

Parliament failed to find a replacement for Church rates, which remained such a bitter source of contention that several Dissenters were imprisoned over this issue during the next two decades. Both in the 1830s and during Russell's prime-ministership after 1846 the Whigs also introduced bills which would allow Jews to sit in parliament but (like many of their more radical proposals) these were turned down by the Lords. [J]

Today the Whig measures seem very moderate. At the time conservative members of the Anglican church judged them extreme. In response to the Irish Church Act, John Keble, John Henry Newman, Hurrell Froude and a group of Oxford clerics began to preach sermons and write tracts attacking state interference in spiritual matters. Thus began the Oxford Movement. It was a High Church revival in that it stressed the Catholic tradition of the Anglican church, insisted that its bishops were spiritually descended from the apostles appointed by Christ and urged that greater emphasis be placed on the sacraments. Divisive though they were, the zeal of the Oxford reformers helped, as did that of numerous rivals in the Evangelical wing, to reinvigorate the Victorian Church – though Newman himself left the Church of England to become a Roman Catholic in 1845. [L–N]

Undoubtedly the reforms helped to 'save' the Church of England, so that by the middle of the century there was little talk of disestablishment. Nevertheless, a census taken of church attendance on 30 March 1851 suggested that for much of the population the legislation was irrelevant. Its compiler, Horace Mann, estimated that on that day only about a half the adults of England and Wales attended a church or chapel; furthermore, he concluded that the absentees were largely from the labouring class. Most modern historians accept the census as evidence that Victorian religious observance was determined by class, while stressing, however, that the lives of most working-class people were affected by religion in one way or another. [O–R]

A Lord Liverpool defends the close link between the Church and the state against any suggestion of change

The principle of the constitution as established in 1688 was essentially Protestant . . . Our ancestors had wisely adopted the principle, that the connexion of a church and a limited monarchy was absolutely essential to the existence of civil liberty and of constitutional government; and in deciding that the king must be Protestant, they had also decided that the government must be Protestant . . . He [Lord Liverpool] could not consent to risk the security of the Protestant constitution established at the Revolution, recollecting the blessings which the country had enjoyed under that constitution, especially through the maintenance of the Protestant religion with a Protestant monarchy and a Protestant parliament.

from a speech in the House of Lords, 17 May 1819

B John Wade's *Black Book* typifies the widespread criticism of the Church in the 1820s and 1830s
To the Church of England, in the abstract, we have no weighty objection to offer; and we should be sorry to see her spiritual functions superseded by those of any other sect by which she is surrounded. Our dislike originates in her extreme oppressiveness on the people, and her unjust dealings towards the most deserving members of her own communion. To the enormous amount of her temporalities [possessions], and abuses in their administration, we particularly demur. It is unseemly, we think, and inconsistent with the very principles and purposes of Christianity, to contemplate lofty prelates with £20,000 or £40,000 a-year, elevated on thrones, living sumptuously in splendid palaces, attended by swarms of menials, gorgeously attired . . . Beneath them are crowds of sinecure dignitaries and incumbents, richly provided with worldly goods, the wealthiest not even obliged to reside among their flocks; and those who reside not compelled to do any one act of duty beyond providing and paying a miserable deputy just enough to keep him from starving. Contrasted with the preceding, is a vast body of poor laborious ministers, doing all the work, and receiving less than the pay of a common bricklayer . . . but the whole assemblage, both rich and poor, paid so as to be a perpetual burden upon the people, and to wage, of necessity, a ceaseless strife with those whom they ought to comfort, cherish, and instruct.

from the *Black Book*, published in 1820–3 and reissued in 1831, 1832 and 1835

C Lord Radnor tells the French writer, de Tocqueville, that in 1833
The number of Dissenters is rapidly increasing; sects are multiplying infinitely . . . [In the Established Church] one finds oneself in fine churches where there are always carpets, comfortable pews, well-dressed people and well-educated preachers. The poor man who is born in the bosom of the Established Church, is made uneasy by the very splendour; his feeling of inferiority takes him to a church where he finds his like in the congregation, and in the preacher a man less superior to himself and one who can say things within his grasp. A great many poor men leave the Established Church for these reasons.

from *Journeys to England and Ireland* by A. de Tocqueville

D The Methodist preacher, Joseph Barker, describes how his father, a weaver, responded to Methodism in the late 18th century
My father got among the Methodists in Kent, and began to be religious. This was the beginning of a new life to him, and he rejoiced in the change very much. Religion brought him into fresh company, gave him new thoughts and new feelings, new loves and new pleasures, new hopes and new work. It was, in truth, a new creation or new birth . . . They [his parents] knew nothing of theology, nothing of controversy. Their simple creed was that there was one God, one Christ, one hope, one religion, one heaven. To love God and all mankind, to shun evil and do good, to go through life with clean hands and pure hearts, rejoicing in the hopes of everlasting blessedness, was all they cared about.

from *The Life of Joseph Barker written by himself* (1880)

E Elizabeth Fry describes some of her strenuous labours as a Quaker minister, work she would not have been able to do in the Church of England
We [she and her sister-in-law] returned home from our journey . . . having been absent just five weeks. We visited several places in the south of Ireland, a good many in Wales, and some in England. I think I never remember taking a journey, in which it was more frequently sealed to my own mind, that we were in our right places; through much difficulty, our way was opened to go, and to continue out. Though I believe we have scripture authority for it – still further confirmed by the internal evidence of the power of the Spirit, and its external results, – yet, I am obliged to walk by faith, rather than sight, in going about, as a woman, in the work of the ministry . . . Generally, when engaged in the ministry, I find such an unction, and so much opening upon Christian doctrine and practice, that after a Meeting, I mostly say in my heart, 'It is the Lord's doing, and marvellous in our eyes.' Such was often the case in this journey.

from Elizabeth Fry's journal, September 1832

F Lord John Russell proposes the Repeal of the Test and Corporation Acts on the main principle
that every man . . . should be at liberty to worship God according to the dictates of his conscience, without being subjected to any penalty or disqualification whatsoever . . . [The Repeal] will be more consonant to the tone and spirit of the age than the existence of those angry yet inefficient and impracticable laws which are a disgrace to the Statute-book.

from a speech in the House of Commons, 26 February 1828

G In a pamphlet addressed to the Lord Chancellor, Dissenters protest against their remaining grievances
No, my Lord, the Dissenters are not satisfied – they *cannot* be satisfied with their present position. They demand the *equality* of citizens. They do not ask to be placed above the Churchman; they cannot submit to be placed beneath him. They claim, that no man shall be the worse, either in *purse*, *reputation*, or *privilege*, on account of his religious opinions. That is what they seek. [After listing their grievances they urge] any government . . . *just to let religion alone*.

from *The Case of the Dissenters* (1833)

H The Revd Sydney Smith was unusual among Anglican clergymen in that he was a Whig and a strong supporter of Roman Catholic Emancipation. This is part of a sermon he preached on 5th November, a traditionally anti-Catholic day in England
I hope in this condemnation of the Catholic religion in which I sincerely join their worst enemies, I shall not be so far mistaken as to have it supposed that I would convey the slightest approbation of any laws which disqualify and incapacitate any class of men for Civil offices on account of religious opinions. I consider all such laws as fatal, and lamentable mistakes in legislation. They are the mistakes of troubled times, and half barbarous ages.

from a letter to Lady Holland, 5 November 1828

I Daniel O'Connell expresses his rage about the grievances of Irish Catholics, which had not been alleviated by Emancipation
He had come down to the House that night in expectation that the attention of English members would be aroused to the condition of Irish people, and that their sense of justice would have impelled them to come to a satisfactory settlement of the question of tithes; but a chill came over him when he saw the benches so empty . . . The truth was that tithes were the great political and agrarian agitators. If they were taken away, disturbance would exist no longer . . . The people of Ireland had determined to pay tithes no longer . . . they had determined to resist them, even to death.

from a speech in the House of Commons, 6 May 1834

J In 1847 Lord John Russell, proposes the removal of discrimination against Jews
on the solid ground that every Englishman, born in the country, is entitled to all the honours and advantages of the British Constitution . . . I believe that the general feeling and, as I conceive, the right and true feeling, to be that religious opinion ought not to bring with it any

penalty or punishment, and that that right and true opinion is rapidly overbearing all prejudice.

His right-wing opponent, Sir Robert Inglis, argues that
the very gentleman whom we saw in his turban under the gallery three or four evenings ago, Rango Bapojee, the vakeel of the late Rajah of Sattara, might as fitly take his place amongst us as the Jew . . . Were the Jews the hereditary inhabitants of this our England? Were they contemporary with the Saxon race, or with the Norman race, or with our Scottish brethren? No, Sir, I repeat it, the remotest ancestors of the present generation of Jews came into England less than two hundred years ago; they came here for their own profit, for their own convenience.

from a debate in the House of Commons, 16 December 1847

K Some years later Mr Gladstone gives his approval to the Church reforms of the 1830s
[Before 1830] our churches and our worship bore in general too conclusive testimony to a frozen indifference. No effort had been made . . . to overtake the religious destitution of the multitudes . . . But between 1831 and 1840, the transformation, which had previously begun, made a progress altogether marvellous . . . The Church of England was . . . roused by the political events which arrived in a quick and rattling succession . . . There was now a general uprising of religious feeling in the Church throughout the land. It saved the Church. Her condition before 1830 could not have borne the scrutinising eye . . . Her rank corruptions must have called down the avenging arm. But it was arrested just in time. Laws were passed to repress gross abuses; and the altering spirit of the clergy seconded, and even outstripped, the laws.

from *Gleanings of Past Years* by W. E. Gladstone (1879)

L In the first *Tract for the Times* John Henry Newman tells his fellow clergymen that their authority rests on the divine commission which Christ gave the Apostles, from whom Anglican bishops are descended
Should the Government and country so far forget their GOD as to cast off the Church, to deprive it of its temporal honours and substance, *on what* will you rest the claim of respect and attention which you make upon your flocks? Hitherto you have been upheld by your birth, your education, your wealth, your connexions; should these secular advantages cease, on what must Christ's ministers depend? . . . Christ has not left His Church without claim of its own upon the attention of men . . . I fear we have neglected the real ground on which our authority is built, – OUR APOSTOLICAL DESCENT.

from *Tracts for the Times* (1833)

M W. F. Hook, Vicar of Leeds from 1837 to 1859, was known as 'the working man's vicar' because of his support for social causes. Here, though, he attributes his increased congregations to his emphasis on Church sacraments and ritual

I do not oppose Dissenters by disputations and wrangling, but I seek to exhibit to the world the Church in all her beauty; let the services of the Church be properly performed, and right-minded people will soon learn to love her.

from *The Life and Letters of W. F. Hook* by W. R. W. Stephens (1878)

N George Eliot describes the influence of Edgar Tryan, a fictional clergyman, who brought to his parish of Milby

that idea of duty, that recognition of something to be lived for beyond the mere satisfaction of self . . . Miss Rebecca Linnet, in quiet attire, with a somewhat excessive solemnity of countenance, teaching at the Sunday-school, visiting the poor, and striving after a standard of purity and goodness, had surely more moral loveliness than in those flaunting peony-days, when she had no other model than the costumes of the heroines in the circulating library . . . Even elderly fathers and mothers, with minds too tough to imbibe much doctrine, were the better for having their hearts inclined towards the new preacher as a messenger from God. They became ashamed, perhaps, of their evil tempers, ashamed of their worldliness, ashamed of their trivial, futile past. The first condition of human goodness is something to love; the second, something to reverence. And this latter precious gift was brought to Milby by Mr Tryan and Evangelicalism.

from *Scenes of Clerical Life* by George Eliot (1857)

O The Religious Census of 1851 gives the number of worshippers in different churches

The Church of England	5,292,551
The Roman Catholics	383,630
The main Protestant Dissenting Churches (Presbyterian, Methodist, Congregationalist, Baptist)	4,536,264
Total Population of England and Wales	17,927,609

Horace Mann explains his findings

While the labouring myriads of our country have been multiplying with our multiplied material prosperity, it cannot, it is feared, be stated that a corresponding increase has occurred in the attendance of this class in our religious edifices. More specially in cities and large towns it is observable how absolutely insignificant a portion of the congregations is composed of artisans. They fill, perhaps, in youth, our National, British, and Sunday Schools, and there receive the elements of a

35

religious education; but, no sooner do they mingle in the active world of labour than, subjected to the constant action of opposing influences, they soon become as utter strangers to religious ordinances as the people of a heathen country.

from the Religious Census of 1851

P A *Punch* cartoon from a series entitled *From the Mining Districts* (1855)

FROM THE MINING DISTRICTS.

AN ATTEMPT AT CONVERTING THE NATIVES.

Assiduous Young Curate. "WELL THEN, I DO HOPE I SHALL HAVE THE PLEASURE OF SEEING BOTH OF YOU NEXT SUNDAY!"

Miner. "OI! THEE MAY'ST COAM IF 'E WULL. WE FOIGHT ON THE CROFT, AND OLD JOE TANNER BRINGS TH' BEER."

Q Among the London poor interviewed by the social investigator, Henry Mayhew, there were not many church-goers. An 18-year-old coster-girl gives her ideas on religion

Father has told me that God made the world, and I've heerd him talk about the first man and woman as was made and lived – it must be more than a hundred years ago – but I don't like to speak on what I don't know. Father, too, has told me about our Saviour what was nailed on a cross to suffer for such poor people as we is. Father has told us, too, about his giving a great many poor people a penny loaf and a bit of fish each, which proves him to have been a very kind gentleman. The Ten Commandments was made by him, I've heerd say, and he performed them too among other miracles. Yes! this is part of what our Saviour tells us. We are to forgive everybody, and do nobody no injury. I don't think I could forgive an enemy if she injured me very much . . . If a gal stole my shawl and didn't return it back or give me the value on it, I couldn't forgive her; but if she told me she lost it off her back, I shouldn't be so hard on her. We poor gals ain't very religious, but we are better than the men. We all of us thanks God for everything – even for a fine day.

from *London Labour and the London Poor* by H. Mayhew (1851)

R A modern historian's view

The great majority of working-class people, neither regular attenders nor total strangers to the churches, considered themselves Christians. Most were married in church; many mothers insisted on being churched after giving birth; most had their babies christened . . . Most working-class children went to Sunday school . . . Children looked forward to the summer treat as one of the high points of the year . . . Many children received religious instruction in church day schools . . . Working-class people also looked to the churches . . . for charity; a constant stream of poor people came to the vicarage door asking for help and they rarely went away empty-handed . . . Working people dealt with the churches on their own terms, taking what they wanted and ignoring the rest. They picked and chose in a similar way among the churches' doctrines and moral teachings . . . What Christianity meant to them was not belief or doctrine but kindness, 'decent behaviour' and doing as you would be done by.

from an article by J. Obelkevich in *Cambridge Social History of Britain* (1990)

Questions

1 How do sources C–E illustrate the attractions of Dissent in the early 19th century?   **(6 marks)**

2 Evaluate the arguments against religious discrimination contained in sources F–J.   **(8 marks)**

3 To what extent do sources A and B bear out Gladstone's description of the unreformed Church in source K? Do you think that he exaggerates the scale of the reforms?   **(10 marks)**

4 In what different ways do sources L–N illustrate the 'altering spirit of the clergy' mentioned by Gladstone in source K?   **(8 marks)**

5 Which of the different types of evidence presented in sources O–R gives the most reliable picture of religious practice among the working classes in the mid-19th century? How would you justify your choice? **(8 marks)**

4 DISCIPLINING PAUPERS

The Whigs did not forget Cobbett's 'hungry and half-starved labourers' [Chapter 2 Source Q]. Even before the Reform Bill was passed they appointed a Royal Commission to inquire into the Poor Law – the means by which poverty was relieved. But there has been much debate about whether the 'great change' which resulted from the inquiry helped or harmed the poor.

The existing system of poor relief dated back to Elizabethan times and was organised by the country's 15,000 parishes. They appointed overseers to deal with applicants, who were only entitled to relief in the parish of their birth. Help could take the form of 'indoor relief', to paupers living in the parish workhouse, or 'outdoor relief', money or goods given to paupers living at home. Since the late 18th century it had become more common to grant outdoor relief. Most parishes in the south followed the 'Speenhamland system': money was granted on the basis of the size of family and the current price of bread. The Poor Law was financed from rates paid by local landowners and tenant farmers. [A–C]

In granting more outdoor relief the parishes were responding to increasing hardship in rural areas. Agricultural labourers had been reduced to desperate straits by the enclosure of common land and by the decline in domestic industry. They were also affected by wage reductions and unemployment resulting from the post-war depression in agriculture. [D]

These causes of poverty are more apparent to historians than they were to most contemporaries, who increasingly tended to blame the Poor Law itself. The influential economist, Thomas Malthus, argued that outdoor relief encouraged idle habits as well as large families, thereby creating more poverty. Benthamite politicians tended to agree and also condemned unsupervised parish administration as inefficient and wasteful. Farmers were alarmed at the soaring poor rates (which in 1832 cost £8.6 million compared to £2 million in the 1780s) and used them as an excuse to pay their employees low wages. Overseers in many parishes began to adopt more stringent methods of determining who was entitled to relief. Some humanitarians pleaded for generosity but economic and moral opinion was hardening against the poor, especially after the widespread agricultural riots of 1830–1. [E–H]

These were the pressures which led the Whigs to appoint a Poor Law Commission, dominated by Benthamites Edwin Chadwick and Nassau Senior, to suggest 'alterations, amendments and improvements'. The Poor Law Report of 1834 duly condemned the entitlement of the able-bodied to outdoor relief, and recommended that it should only be paid to old and sick paupers who had no families to maintain them. Relief was instead to be given in 'well-regulated' workhouses, where conditions should be harsher than those normally prevailing outside so as to make the workhouse 'less eligible' [less likely to be chosen]. The poor would then be deterred from applying for relief and would support themselves by their own labours. To make the system more efficient parishes were to be grouped into Unions run by elected Guardians and a central Board of three Commissioners was to supervise them. These recommendations were the basis of the Poor Law Amendment Bill of 1834, which was passed through parliament with little opposition from Whigs or Tories. [I–L]

The implementation of the act was not as easy as its passing. It is true that by 1837 the administrative reorganisation had been completed and many suitably grim workhouses had been built in the rural south and midlands. But in some areas there had been spirited and occasionally violent resistance. This foreshadowed the systematic opposition which the commissioners met when they began to establish Unions in the industrial north. By then a severe trade depression was causing unemployment and wage reductions; workers feared that they would be incarcerated in workhouses where their families would be split up. Worried by the ferocity of the anti-Poor Law campaign (in which women played a more significant part than in any previous protest movement), the government slowed down the creation of Unions and the building of workhouses. The authorities in the north found that they had to continue outdoor relief payments. But the anger stirred up by the new law did not disappear. As Thomas Carlyle recognised [Chapter 1, source K], it helped to fuel the Chartist movement in the 1840s. [M–P]

Meanwhile, rural Guardians reported to the government that the act was working as intended. Modern research indicates, however, that in practice they were using their discretion and bending the rules, not least because it was cheaper to grant minimal outdoor relief than to maintain people in workhouses. Thus in 1850 only 110,000 paupers, out a total of 1 million, were workhouse inmates; many of these were the old and sick who had nowhere else to go. They had to put up with the regimentation and the psychological cruelty meant to discourage the able-bodied poor.

The act succeeded in that it brought down Poor Law expenditure from £7 million in 1834 to £4.5 million in 1844. It also created a lasting fear of the workhouse and made poverty seem a disgrace. After the act, as before it, poor people continued to manage as best they could, relying more on the help of family and neighbourhood than on statutory aid. [Q–S]

A Cambridge was one area which used a scale of relief based on the price of bread

The Churchwardens and Overseers of the Poor are requested to regulate the incomes of such persons as may apply to them for relief or employment, according to the price of fine bread; namely,

A single woman, the price of		3½ quarten loaves per week	
A single man		4½	"
A man and his wife		8	"
"	and one child	9½	"
"	and two children	11	"
"	and three "	13	"

Man, wife, four children and upwards, at the price of 2½ quarten loaves per head per week.

It will be necessary to add to the above incomes in all cases of sickness or other kinds of distress; and particularly of such persons or families who deserve encouragement by their good behaviour, whom parish officers should mark both by commendation and reward.

quoted in the Poor Law Report of 1834

B In 1818 the parish vestry meeting of Tysoe placed conditions on the receipt of outdoor relief

It was unanimously agreed that all men and boys who are out of employ shall walk from the Coal Barn as far as the Red Lion Inn in Middle Tysoe, or stand in the gateway near the Barn the full space of ten hours on each day . . . and it is also agreed that if any person enter any house during the ten hours he or she shall receive no pay from the Parish.

from *Joseph Ashby of Tysoe* by M. K. Ashby (1961)

C The following story, reported by one of the Poor Law Commissioners (who disapproved of the outcome), provides insight into how the old system of poor relief operated

A pauper named Sutton returned to the parish with his wife and child, having been away for some time, and applied for relief and clothes for himself and family. The overseers, suspecting that he possessed clothes, managed to get him and his wife out of the room, keeping his little girl in, and then asked the child where her Sunday frock was. She answered that it was locked up in a box at Cambridge with other things. Here the mother came in to call the girl out, but the overseers would not let her go, whereupon the father came in with a bludgeon, and seized the child by the arm. The overseers held her, but the father pulling her so as to hurt her, they let her go, and he took her out and beat her violently. He then returned, demanding relief, which they refused. He then abused them dreadfully, threatening to rip up one, burn the town etc., and behaved with such violence that they were compelled to have him handcuffed and his legs tied, and he was wheeled in a barrow to the magistrate, where they charged him with assault. The magistrate asked whether they could swear they were in bodily fear of Sutton, and they replying that they were not, he dismissed the charge and ordered Sutton relief.

from Appendix A to the Poor Law Report of 1834

D Cobbett sheds light on one of the causes of rural poverty by describing an unusually prosperous area

I have observed, in this country, and especially near Worcester, that the working people seem to be better off than in many other parts, one cause of which is, I dare say, that *glove-manufacturing*, which cannot be carried on by *fire* or by *wind* or by *water*, is, therefore carried on by the *hands* of human beings. It gives work to women and children as well as to men; and that work is . . . done in *their* cottages, and amidst the fields and hop-gardens, where the husbands and sons must live, in order to raise the food and the drink and the wool . . . If this glove-making were to cease, many of these women and children, now *not* upon the parish, must instantly be upon the parish . . . Where the manufacturing . . . is performed by females at their *own homes*, and where the earnings come *in aid of the man's* wages; in such case the misery cannot be so great.

from *Rural Rides* by W. Cobbett (1830)

E The explanation for poverty given by economist Thomas Malthus was much quoted in the early 19th century

I feel no doubt whatever that the parish laws of England have contributed to raise the price of provisions and to lower the real price of labour. They have therefore contributed to impoverish that class of people whose only possession is their labour. It is also difficult to suppose that they have not powerfully contributed to generate that carelessness and want of frugality observable among the poor, so contrary to the disposition frequently to be remarked among petty tradesmen and small farmers. The labouring poor, to use a vulgar expression, seem always to live from hand to mouth. Their present wants employ their whole attention, and they seldom think of the future. Even when they have an opportunity of saving they seldom exercise it, but all that is beyond their present necessities goes, generally speaking, to the ale-house. The poor-laws of England may therefore be said to diminish both the power and the will to save among the common people, and thus to weaken one of the strongest incentives to sobriety and industry, and consequently to happiness.

from *An Essay on the Principle of Population* by T. Malthus (1798)

F A Cambridgeshire smallholder defends outdoor relief

We have heard of the hardships endured by the West Indian slaves, –

can they surpass the hardships endured by the British labourers? Yet these are the men, to whom, under Divine Providence, we owe the bread we eat . . . Think you, if they had no poor laws to protect them when out of employ, that they would – that they could – suffer their wives and their little ones to perish with hunger? Let every one whose eyes this may meet, supply his own answer. I mention these things, because there are to be found, those who are so destitute of sympathy for the labouring portion of the community, as to be hostile to the poor laws, and to wish to annul them altogether.

from *A Peasant's Voice to Landowners* by John Denson (1830)

**G W. H. Hudson's interviews with old Wiltshire farm labourers provide
the basis of his explanation for the agricultural riots of 1830–1**
I can understand how it came about that these poor labourers, poor spiritless slaves as they had been made by long years of extremest poverty and systematic oppression, rose at last against their hard masters and smashed the agricultural machines, and burnt ricks and broke into houses to destroy and plunder their contents. It was a desperate, a mad adventure . . . but oppression had made them mad; the introduction of the threshing machines was but the last straw . . . It was not merely the fact that the wages of a strong man were only seven shillings a week at the outside, a sum barely sufficient to keep him and his family from starvation and rags (as a fact it was not enough, and but for a little poaching and stealing he could not have lived), but it was customary, especially on the small farms, to get rid of the men after the harvest and leave them to exist the best way they could during the bitter winter months. Thus every village, as a rule, had its dozen or twenty or more men thrown out each year . . . and besides these there were the aged and weaklings and the lads who had not yet got a place. The misery of these out-of-work labourers was extreme. They would go to the woods and gather faggots of dead wood, which they would try to sell in the villages; but there were few who could afford to buy of them; and at night they would skulk about the fields to rob a swede or two to satisfy the cravings of hunger.

from *A Shepherd's Life* by W. H. Hudson (1910)

**H But the Poor Law Commissioners blame the farm labourers' riots on
the system of outdoor relief**
It appears from all our returns, especially from the replies to the rural queries, that in every district, the discontent of the labouring classes is proportioned to the money dispensed in poor rates, or in voluntary charities . . . The violence of most of the mobs seems to have arisen from an idea that all their privations arose from the cupidity or fraud of those entrusted with the management of the fund provided for the poor

. . . Whatever addition is made to allowances under these circumstances excites the expectation of still further allowances, increases the conception of the extent of the right, and ensures proportionate disappointment and hatred if that expectation is not fulfilled.

from the Poor Law Report of 1834

I The Poor Law Commissioners explain how workhouse conditions will be rendered more 'irksome' than those of the independent labourer
It is not by means of labour alone that the principle is applicable, nor does it imply that the food or comforts of the pauper should approach the lowest point at which existence may be maintained. Although the workhouse food be more ample in quantity and better in quality than that of which the labourer's family partakes, and the house in other respects superior to the cottage, yet the strict discipline of well-regulated workhouses, and in particular the restrictions to which the inmates are subject in respect to the use of acknowledged luxuries, such as fermented liquors and tobacco, are intolerable to the indolent and disorderly, while to the aged, the feeble and other proper objects of relief, the regularity and discipline render the workhouse a place of comparative comfort.

from the Poor Law Report of 1834

J The Commissioners recommend diets for the paupers; women's rations are shown in brackets and breakfast is the same each day
Sundays, Tuesdays and Thursdays:
    Breakfast   6 (5) oz. bread, 1½ pints gruel
    Dinner   5 oz. cooked meat, ½ pound potatoes
    Supper   6 (5) oz. bread, 1½ pints broth
Mondays, Wednesdays and Saturdays:
    Dinner   1½ pints soup
    Supper   6 (5) oz. bread, 2 oz. cheese
Fridays:
    Dinner   14 (12) oz. suet or rice pudding
    Supper   6 (5) oz. bread, 2 oz. cheese

from the first Annual Report of the Poor Law Commissioners (1835)

K Writer, Harriet Martineau, was encouraged by the government to popularise the principles of the new Poor Law in simply written stories
The next man who applied declared that he and his young wife must starve if their five shillings were withheld, and made no scruple about entering the [work]house, for which an order was immediately

L The Commissioners recommend a suitable plan for a Union workhouse to contain 300 inmates

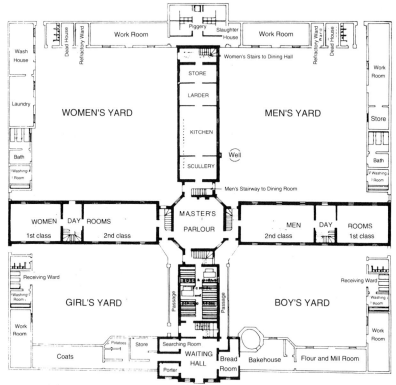

Ground floor of the Poor Law Commissioners' recommended plan for a workhouse to contain 300 paupers : designed by Sampson Kempthorne (from the First Annual Report of the Poor Law Commissioners, 1835).

supplied. A number of idle persons followed his example, knowing that it was considered no bad lot to live in the Hurst workhouse, where the people had hitherto been allowed to do pretty much what they pleased. **They are taken aback by the workhouse uniform, the separation of man and wife, the hard labour and the prohibition on beer and tobacco. So the next morning** they rushed through the portal, with ideas about pauperism very different from what they had had when they entered twenty-four hours before. The few whom they left behind repaired to their work with a heavy heart, thankful to be saved from starvation; but hoping not long to owe their subsistence to legal charity.

from *Poor Law and Paupers Illustrated* by H. Martineau (1833)

M The new law inspired William Wordsworth to write a postscript to his poems of rural life, *Lyrical Ballads*. In it he defends

a right in the people (not to be gainsaid by utilitarians and economists) to public support when, from any cause, they may be unable to support themselves . . . That principle . . . is indispensable for England, upon whose coast families are perpetually deprived of their support by shipwreck, and large masses of men are so liable to be thrown out of their ordinary means of gaining bread, by changes in commercial intercourse, subject mainly or solely to the will of foreign powers; by new discoveries in arts and manufactures; and by reckless laws, in conformity with theories of political economy, which, whether right or wrong in the abstract, have proved a scourge to tens of thousands, by the abruptness with which they have been carried into practice.

from Postscript to *Lyrical Ballads* (1835–6 edition)

N Fergus O'Connor's newspaper, the *Northern Star*, reports one of many attacks by the Revd J. R. Stephens on the Poor Law. (Both these men were Chartists)

And if this damnable law, which violated all the laws of God, was continued, and all means of peaceably putting an end to it had been made in vain, then, in the words of their banner, 'for children and wife we'll war to the knife'. If the people who produce all wealth could not be allowed, according to God's word, to have the kindly fruits of the earth which they had . . . raised by the sweat of their brow, then war to the knife with their enemies who were the enemies of God. If the musket and the pistol, the sword and the pike were of no avail, let the women take the scissors, the child the pin or needle. If all failed, then the firebrand – aye the firebrand – the firebrand, I repeat. The palace shall be in flames . . . If the cottage is not permitted to be the abode of man and wife, and if the smiling infant is to be dragged from a father's arms and a mother's bosom, it is because these hell-hounds of commissioners have set up the command of their master the devil, against our God.

from *Northern Star*, 6 January 1838

O At a public meeting held by the women of Elland (Yorkshire) in February 1838 Mrs Grasby moves a resolution against the Act

They might be asked why women should interfere in public matters. She would answer at once, it was a woman's duty to be there; for women had more to fear from this bill than men. (Cheers) Could she, the mother, be taught to forget her suckling child? No mother could; therefore . . . she would oppose that law and she called upon her sisters now before her to follow her example. (Tremendous cheering) Women have still more to do with this cruel measure than men. Their feelings were more susceptible and the pangs of being separated from those to whom they had been used to look for support, and from the children of their own bearing were more severe, she believed, than it was possible for men to feel. (Loud cheers) They ought also to resist it from a sense of duty. It was their duty to be, each one, a helpmate to her husband – to soothe his sorrows, but this law prevented her from being able to do so . . . She exhorted them fearlessly, women as they were, to address the Queen, and if they should do so unsuccessfully, still not to be desponding, but boldly and patiently persevere in their opposition, and all obstacles would be overcome. (Great cheering)

The following month in Elland

The female Reformers mustered in strong numbers . . . and treated the Guardians to a roll in the snow; and one of them, a stout portly man, offered to treat them to a gill of ale each if they would allow him to escape; but the bribe would not do. The women are determined to give every resistance to this infernal measure.

from reports in *Northern Star* (17 February and 3 March 1838)

P Social commentator, William Cooke Taylor, describes the impact of the 1840s trade depression on Colne, Lancashire

Out of a population of 53,000, no less than 13,000 were receiving parish relief; the poor-rates had risen from 3 shillings to 10 shillings in the pound; the relief granted was esteemed by the paupers so inadequate to their wants, that the relieving officer in one district was obliged to be protected by a military guard . . . Chartism was advancing with fearful rapidity in this part of the country.

from *Notes on a Tour in the Manufacturing Districts of Lancashire* by W. Cooke Taylor (1842)

Q Lucy Luck, a straw-plait worker born in 1848, remembers what happened when her father deserted his wife and four small children

My father I will sum up in a very few words. I had been given to understand he was an experienced brick-layer by trade, but he was a drunkard and a brute. After bringing his wife and children to poverty and starvation he deserted and left my mother to face the world alone as best she could with her family, and she never heard of him again. What could my mother do but apply to the parish? – which she did, and the answer they gave her was, 'You must go to the workhouse, and the Guardians will find your husband.' . . . Now the workhouse belonging to Tring was five miles away, and some sort of conveyance was provided for my crippled sister, but my mother had to get there as best she could with us others . . . [When] we got to a school not far from the Union . . . my mother sat down on the steps with one of us on each side of her and one in her arms, crying bitterly over us before she took us into the Union.

from *Useful Toil: Autobiographies of Working People* by J. Burnett (1974)

R Henry Mayhew interviews a London street-seller of tape and cotton who was supporting her sick husband
'The overseer came to see if my old man was fit to be removed to the workhouse. The doctor gave me a certificate that he was not, and then the relieving officer gave me a shilling and a loaf of bread . . . What shocked him [her husband] most was that I was obligated in his old age to go and ask for relief at the parish. You see, he was always a spiritful man, and it hurted him sorely that he should come to this at last, and this for the first time in his lifetime . . . and it does hurt him every day to think that he must be buried by the parish after all. He was always so proud, you see.' . . . The day after the above was written, the poor old man died. He was buried out of funds sent to the *Morning Chronicle*, and his wife received some few pounds to increase her stock; but in a few months the poor old woman went mad and is now, I believe, the inmate of one the pauper lunatic-asylums.

from *London Labour and the London Poor* by H. Mayhew (1851)

S A modern historian sums up the impact of the new Poor Law
Once established, the basic philosophy of the poor relief system, formulated in the 1830s and 1840s, persisted almost until the end of the century. The stigma of pauperism was inculcated from an early stage, and only those who could manage in no other way resorted to Poor Law assistance. So while the 1834 Act may have fostered self-dependence – it boosted friendly society membership, for example – it failed to recognise the genuine needs of the poor.

from *The Rural World* by P. Horn (1980)

Questions

1 What can be learned from sources A–C about how the old Poor Law worked? **(6 marks)**

2 Use sources D–H to discuss the causes of poverty in the early 19th century. **(8 marks)**

3 Use sources I–L to demonstrate how the principle of 'less eligibility' was meant to work. **(8 marks)**

4 Evaluate the arguments used to attack the new Poor Law in sources M–O. **(8 marks)**

5 To what extent do sources P–R bear out the points made in source S? **(10 marks)**

5 PUNISHING FELONS

The workhouses established by the new Poor Law were often referred to as 'Bastilles', a nickname derived from the prison attacked and torn down by French revolutionaries in 1789. Was there really any resemblance between workhouses and prisons? This chapter should help to answer that question.

The old penal system of the late 18th and early 19th centuries was often referred to as 'The Bloody Code' because of the large number and variety of offences which were punishable by death – about 225 by the end of the Napoleonic Wars. Death was by public hanging. In practice the code was not as bloody as it looks; many of the statutes had fallen into disuse and of those condemned to death a high proportion had their sentences commuted to transportation. Physical punishments still inflicted at this time were whipping, the pillory and the stocks. Imprisonment had been relatively rare in the 18th century but was becoming more common. There was no government control over prisons, discipline in which varied a great deal. Conditions were usually squalid, but, for those who could afford to pay the gaolers, prison life could be reasonably comfortable. [A, F, G]

Although the English system could be compared favourably to the police despotism which existed elsewhere in Europe, reformers criticised the code in various ways. Some attacked over-dependence on the death penalty as being not only inhumane but also ineffective. There was a growing school of thought, influenced by prison reformers like John Howard and Elizabeth Fry, which held that the main aim of imprisonment should be the rehabilitation rather than the punishment of the offender. Thus gaols should be humanely but strictly regulated on a rational basis so that their inmates would spend their time in 'reflection' and possibly 'repentance' rather than 'gaming, drunkenness, quarrelling, profaneness and obscenity'. The idea gained ground that in an age when social discipline was breaking down the state should intervene to supply this need. [B, H, I]

Before 1820 a few county gaols had already adopted a system of separate confinement and an experimental and unsuccessful 'Panopticon' (the kind of gaol advocated by Bentham in which the prisoners were constantly watched) had been built at Millbank in London. But it was during the three decades after 1820 that the penal system was rationalised and centralised in Benthamite fashion. The long campaign of Whigs like Romilly and Mackintosh to reduce the number of capital offences had some effect during the 1820s, though the Tory Home Secretary, Robert

Peel, insisted on retaining the death penalty for many crimes including forgery. Largely on the initiative of some of the new MPs voted into parliament after the 1832 Reform Act, the process was accelerated so that by 1837 there were only eight capital offences; executions continued to be carried out in public until 1868. The frequency of tranportation increased accordingly, accounting for a third of all sentences by the mid 1830s. Doubts were then raised in Britain and Australia about its effectiveness as a punishment, especially for women. Its use declined, though it was not abolished until 1867. [C, D, E, J]

Reformers pinned their hopes increasingly on the penitentiary, which would combine terror with humanity. Peel's Gaols Act of 1823 spelled out regulations to improve the health, education, work, religion and categorisation of prisoners, though these were not effectively enforced since there was no government inspection. In the 1830s discipline was tightened: diets were pared down and the newly-invented treadmill was introduced as the ideal form of hard labour (though it had its critics). The rule of silence was introduced so that, by 1835, 19 counties had banned all speech and gesture among prison inmates. Elizabeth Fry was worried that these changes meant 'more cruelty in the gaols' than ever. But the rising crime rate (or perhaps the higher number of prosecutions resulting from the establishment of urban police forces after 1829) spurred magistrates and politicians on to make the prisons efficient. An inspectorate was established in 1835 and gaols were made accountable to the Home Office. [K–L]

The culmination of these 'reforms' was the building of Pentonville gaol, opened in 1842 as a model prison to operate the 'separate system'. Prisoners were well fed and housed, according to Henry Mayhew, in 'wondrous and perfectly Dutch-like cleanliness'; they spent their days in total isolation and silence performing long hours of useful labour in their cells. During exercise periods they wore peaked masks so that they could not see other inmates. In the chapel, an essential part of the treatment, they were herded into separate boxes (with slanting seats, so that they had to support themselves with braced legs) from which they could see the chaplain but not each other. Punishments were imposed on those who would not willingly comply with this regime: bread and water diet, pitch dark cells and hard labour. Pentonville was judged a great success and by 1850 there were 20 similar prisons, though old habits survived in many others (most shamefully in the prison ships or hulks, 'the despair of all reformers', said Mayhew). Exemplary though it was generally thought to be, the separate system always had its critics, among whom were Mayhew himself, Carlyle and Dickens.It survived until the 1870s. [M–Q]

Contemporaries congratulated themselves on what had been achieved and their optimistic opinion has generally been accepted. Recently, however, historians have challenged the received wisdom. Michael Ignatieff, for example, stresses the similarities between model prisons and other new institutions such as workhouses, factories and monitorial schools, all of which were seeking to control their inmates. [R] The falling crime rate of the 1850s is now attributed not so much to the penal reforms of the 1830s and 1840s as to the improved living standards of the mid-century.

A Statistics reveal the difference between theory and practice in sentences passed at the Old Bailey

	Capital convictions	Executions
1795–1804		
Burglary	168	23
Forgery	61	40
Highway Robbery	127	22
Murder	20	18
1804–1815		
Burglary	226	18
Forgery	84	47
Highway Robbery	196	17
Murder	26	26

from *Crime and Society in England 1750–1900* by C. Emsley (1987)

B Whig MP Samuel Romilly argues in parliament for the repeal of laws imposing the death penalty for stealing goods to the value of £5 from a shop or goods to the value of 40 shillings from a house. His bills passed through the Commons but were rejected in the Lords

There is probably no country in the world in which so many and so great a variety of human actions are punishable with loss of life as in England. These sanguinary statutes, however, are not carried into execution. For some time past the sentence of death has not been executed on more than a sixth part of the persons on whom it has been pronounced . . . This leniency I am very far from censuring; on the contrary I applaud the wisdom as well as the humanity of it . . . It is sufficient, however, to say of these laws, that it is impossible that they should be executed; and, that, instead of preventing, they have multiplied crimes, the very crimes they were intended to repress, and others no less alarming to society, perjury, and the obstructing of the administration of justice . . . [Moreover] they form a kind of standard of cruelty, to justify every harsh and excessive exercise of authority.

from a speech in the House of Commons, 1811

C Peel's cautious approach to the abolition of the death penalty is shown in this speech introducing some of his amendments to the criminal law

The law which makes it an offence punishable with death to steal in a dwelling-house to the amount of 40 shillings, extends at present to all outhouses . . . It is intended to except for the future from the operation of this law, so far as regards capital punishment, the stealing in all outhouses which are not connected with the dwelling-house by some internal communication.

from a speech in the House of Commons, 1826.

D Figures showing the effects of Tory and Whig legislation

Ten-year period	Av. number of capital convictions per annum	Av. number of executions per annum	Av. number of executions for murder per annum
1805–14	443	66	13
1815–24	1073	89	16
1825–34	1218	53	12
1835–44	199	13	10
1845–54	57	9	9

from *Crime and Society in England* by C. Emsley (1987)

E Thackeray went to the public hanging of the murderer Courvoisier in 1840, and was more shocked than he expected to be

As the clock began to strike, an immense sway and movement swept over that vast dense crowd. They were all uncovered directly [they removed their hats], and a great murmur arose, more awful, bizarre, and indescribable than any sound I had ever before heard. Women and children began to shriek horribly . . . The scaffold stood before us, tenantless and black; the black chain was hanging down ready from the beam . . .

Courvoisier bore his punishment like a man, and walked very firmly. He was dressed in a new black suit, as it seemed: his shirt was open. His arms were tied in front of him. He opened his hands in a helpless kind of way, and clasped them once or twice together. He turned his head here and there, and looked about him for an instant with a wild, imploring look. His mouth was contracted into a sort of pitiful smile. He went and placed himself at once under the beam, with his face towards St Sepulchre's. The tall, grave man in black twisted him around swiftly in the other direction, and, drawing from his pocket a nightcap, pulled it tight over the patient's head and face. I am not ashamed to say that I could look no more, but shut my eyes as the last dreadful act was going on, which sent this wretched guilty soul into the presence of God . . .

I must confess . . . that the sight has left on my mind an extraordinary feeling of terror and shame. It seems to me that I have been abetting an act of frightful wickedness and violence, performed by one set of men against their fellows; and I pray to God that it may soon be out of the power of any man in England to witness such a hideous and degrading sight.

from *Going to See a Man Hanged* by W. M. Thackeray (1840)

F Lincoln County Gaol was one of the earliest model prisons. John Howard describes it in its pre-reform days
two vaulted dungeons for criminals, eight feet high, both dirty and offensive . . . two rooms with beds for felons who can pay for them . . . [Felons allowed] each weekly 8 lb bread, and 2d for beef; in common yearly £2 for coals, £2 for straw and £2 for oatmeal . . . Every prisoner that will eat at the first table to pay 5 shillings a week for his lodging and diet having three meals a day.

from *The State of the Prisons* by J. Howard (1777)

G In 1820 Samuel Bamford was sentenced to 12 months imprisonment for his participation in radical protest. He served his time in the same unreformed Lincoln gaol but was lucky enough to enjoy its better conditions
A number of my friends at Middleton bestirred themselves, and besides making a present collection, they put down their names for a regular monthly contribution so long as I remained in prison, and thenceforward I received from them one pound a month.
Thus he shared with a fellow Radical
a very pleasant room, with a fire-grate, cupboards for victuals, and places to put coals, potatoes, or other matters in. We both had iron bedsteads, and very comfortably I slept, considering the circumstances.
Later on his wife was allowed to stay in the gaol with him in a room which was 'coloured and cleaned' for their use.

from *Passages in the Life of a Radical* by S. Bamford (1844)

H John Howard explains what he means by prison reform
It may be said, that from the many conveniences suggested in the structure of Gaols, and the removal of those hardships which rendered them so terrible, the dread of being confined in them will in great measure be taken off, and the lower classes of people will find them more comfortable places of residence than their own houses. But let it be considered, in the first place, that although I have indeed recommended such attentions in the construction and management as may free them from the diseases and hardships under which they have laboured, I have proposed nothing to give them an air of elegance, or pleasantness . . . Then, with respect to the more humane treatment of the prisoners in the articles of food, lodging, and the like, I venture to

assert, that if to it be joined such strict regulations in preventing all dissipation and riotous amusement, as I have inculcated, confinement in a prison, though it may cease to be destructive to health and morals, will not fail to be sufficiently irksome and disagreeable, especially to the idle and profligate.

from *The State of the Prisons* by J. Howard (1777)

I The Quaker philanthropist, Elizabeth Fry, concentrates on the special problems of women in Newgate Prison where
we were witnesses to the dreadful proceedings that went forward, on the female side of the prison; the begging, swearing, gaming, fighting, singing, dancing, dressing-up in men's clothes; scenes too bad to be described, so that we did not think it suitable to admit young persons with us.
In 1817 she and eleven other women set up an Association for the Improvement of the Female Prisoners in Newgate
to provide for the clothing, the instruction, and the employment of the women; to introduce them to a knowledge of the Holy Scriptures, and to form in them, as much as possible, those habits of order, sobriety, and industry, which may render them docile and peaceable whilst in prison, and respectable when they leave it.
They did much good work in Newgate and Fry was convinced that
if there were a prison fitted up for us, which we might visit as inspectors – if employment were found for our women, little or no communication allowed with the city, and room given to class them with females . . . only – if there were a thousand of the unruly women, they would be in excellent order in one week.

from evidence given to a Committee of the House of Commons, 1818

J A government report on transportation makes shocking reading even today. After arrival most female convicts were 'assigned' to families as servants
In respectable families the condition of convict women, as respects their food, clothing, and indulgences, is much the same as that of women servants in this country. Their general conduct, according to the testimony of every witness, examined before your Committee, is (to use the words of Sir E. Parry) 'as bad as anything could well be;' he could 'hardly conceive of anything worse.' At times they are excessively ferocious, and the tendency of assignment is to render them still more profligate; they are all of them, with scarcely an exception, drunken and abandoned prostitutes; and even were any of them inclined to be well-conducted, the disproportion of sexes in the penal colonies is so great, that they are exposed to irresistible temptations; for instance, in a private family, in the interior of either colony [New South Wales or Van

Diemen's Land] a convict woman, frequently the only one in the service, perhaps in the neighbourhood, is surrounded by a number of depraved characters, to whom she becomes an object of constant pursuit and solicitation; . . . she either commits some offence, for which she is returned to the Government; or she becomes pregnant, in which case she is sent to the factory, to be there confined at the expense of the Government; at the expiration of the period of confinement or punishment, she is reassigned, and again goes through the same course; such is too generally the career of convict women, even in respectable families.

from the Molesworth Report on Transportation, 1838

K Sydney Smith (a magistrate as well as a clergyman) defends the use of the treadmill for convicted prisoners
The labour of the treadmill is irksome, dull and monotonous, and disgusting to the last degree. A man does not see his work, does not know what he is doing, what progress he is making; there is no room for art, contrivance, ingenuity, and superior human skill – all which are the cheering circumstances of human labour . . . The treader does nothing but tread . . . he is turned at once from a rational being . . . and put upon a level with a rush of water or a puff of steam . . . Nothing can be more excellent than this kind of labour for those persons to whom you mean to make labour as irksome as possible; . . . The treadmill, after trial, is certainly a very excellent method of punishment, as far as we are as yet acquainted with its effects.

from an article in *Edinburgh Review* (1822)

L The writer Charles Lamb uses irony to cast doubt on the new invention
Incompetent my song to raise
To its just height thy praise,
Great Mill!
That by thy motion proper,
(No thanks to wind, or sail, or working rill,)
Grinding that stubborn corn, the Human will,
Turn'st out men's consciences
That were begrimed before, as clean and sweet
As flour from purest wheat,
Into thy hopper.
All reformation short of thee but nonsense is,
Or human, or divine.

from *Ode to the Tread-Mill* by C. Lamb (1825)

THE CHAPEL, ON THE "SEPARATE SYSTEM," IN PENTONVILLE PRISON, DURING DIVINE SERVICE.

M The chapel in the new Pentonville prison

N The Earl of Chichester, one of the commissioners appointed to superintend Pentonville, extols its virtues

Human nature is so constituted that when a man has been long addicted to a life of crime or sensual indulgence it requires a severe affliction to force him to reflect – he must be . . . deprived of those sources of animal pleasure and excitement which have hitherto enabled him to silence his conscience and to shut out from his mind all thoughts of the future – there must be something external to afflict, to break down his spirit, some bodily suffering or distress of mind, before the still small voice will be heard and the man brought to himself.

from a letter to the Home Secretary, 1856

O Henry Mayhew visited all the prisons of London before writing a very detailed account of them. He had mixed feelings about the separate system. He judges both it and the silent system

an eminent improvement upon the old . . . system of our prisons . . . both [of which were] instituted with the kindest possible intentions towards the criminals themselves . . . [It] is the preferable of these two modes of prison government, were it not that the separate system is found to be so dangerous to the mental health of those subject to it . . . We have . . . shown that, whilst the average ratio of insanity from 1843 to 1851 was 5.8 lunatics per annum, to every 10,000 of the gross prison population throughout England and Wales, still, at Pentonville, the average yearly proportion of lunacy . . . was 62.0 per 10,000 prisoners . . . Now, as the driving of a man mad forms no part of his original sentence, it is clear that prison authorities have no earthly right to submit a prisoner to a course of discipline, which, if long protracted, would have the effect of depriving him of his reason.

from *The Criminal Prisons of London* by H. Mayhew (1861)

P After visiting a model prison where the inmates enjoyed 'perfect and thorough cleanliness' and 'superlative' food, Carlyle writes this spirited attack on all prison reform

Howard abated the Jail-Fever; but it seems to me he has been the innocent cause of a far more distressing fever which rages high just now; what we may call the Benevolent-Platform Fever. Howard is to be regarded as the unlucky fountain of that tumultuous frothy ocean-tide of benevolent sentimentality, 'abolition of punishment', all-absorbing 'prison-discipline', and general morbid sympathy, instead of hearty hatred for scoundrels . . . Yes, my friends, scoundrel is scoundrel: that remains for ever a fact; and there exists not in the earth whitewash that can make the scoundrel a friend of this universe; he remains an enemy if you spent your life in whitewashing him.

from *Model Prisons* by T. Carlyle (1850)

Q In Dickens's novel, David Copperfield and his friend Traddles visit a London prison at the invitation of their old schoolmaster Mr Creakle who is now running it and wants to show them

'the only true system of prison discipline; the only unchallengeable way of making sincere and lasting converts and penitents – which is by solitary confinement.' In the course of the visit they are shown model prisoners, Numbers Twenty Seven and Twenty Eight, the former of whom was their old acquaintance, Uriah Heep.

'Well, Twenty Seven,' said Mr. Creakle, mournfully admiring him. 'How do you find yourself today?'

'I am very umble, sir!' replied Uriah Heep.

'You are always so, Twenty Seven,' said Mr. Creakle.

Here another gentleman asked, with extreme anxiety: 'Are you quite comfortable?'

'Yes, I thank you sir!' said Uriah Heep, looking in that direction. 'Far more comfortable here than ever I was outside. I see my follies now, sir. That's what makes me comfortable.'

[On leaving, Copperfield concludes that] it would have been in vain to represent to such a man as the worshipful Mr. Creakle, that Twenty Seven and Twenty Eight were perfectly consistent and unchanged . . . that the hypocritical knaves were just the subjects to make that sort of profession in such a place; that they knew the market-value at least as well as we did, in the immediate service it would do them when they were expatriated . . . .We left them to their system and themselves and went home wondering.

from *David Copperfield* by Charles Dickens (1850)

R A modern historian has reservations about the new penitentiaries, which he brackets with 'reformed' lunatic asylums, workhouses and hospitals

In each environment, the poor were to be 'cured' of immorality, disease, insanity, or crime, as well as related defects of body and mind, by isolation, exhortations, and regimens of obedience training.

In the penitentiary, the agency of cure was contrition. Yet the anguish of guilt could only be aroused, the reformers realised, in an environment whose self-evident humaneness confirmed the moral authority of the state and forced prisoners to recognize their culpability. Solitary confinement appeared to offer this perfect reconciliation of humanity and terror. It epitomized the liberal utopia of a punishment so rational that offenders would punish themselves in the soundless, silent anguish of their own minds . . .

In the Victorian philanthropic tradition, prisoners were not the only ones whose right to be treated as human beings was made conditional on their submission to moral improvement. No attempt to raise the housing, educational, or sanitary standard of the poor was made without an accompanying attempt to colonize their minds. In this tradition, humanitarianism was inextricably linked to the practice of domination.

from *A Just Measure of Pain* by M. Ignatieff (1978)

Questions

1 To what extent does source A support Romilly's arguments on capital punishment in source B? Do sources C–E show such arguments to have been influential? **(8 marks)**

2 How can the practices revealed in sources F, G and J be criticised in the light of the principles demonstrated in sources H and I? **(8 marks)**

3 Using sources K and L construct arguments which could have been used in the 19th century for and against the use of the treadmill as a method of prison discipline. **(6 marks)**

4 How effectively are the principles on which the separate system was based (as illustrated in sources M and N) called into question by the writers of sources O, P, and Q? **(8 marks)**

5 In the light of the comments of Ignatieff (source R), how much improvement do you think was brought about by penal reform in the first half of the 19th century? **(10 marks)**

6 EDUCATING THE POOR

Whenever anyone was due to be hanged in the early 19th century there was a brisk trade in illustrated broadsides telling the story of the crime. Inexpensive religious tracts also abounded at this time. The spread of such cheap street literature suggests some reading ability among the poor though it is difficult to establish how many were literate. The most certain evidence available is the number of brides and grooms able to sign the marriage register, though clearly a signature does not necessarily denote real literacy. On the basis of such evidence historians now think that, even before there was any state provision of education, a surprisingly high proportion of working men and women was reasonably literate. [A]

Some children learned to read at home and many also received more formal teaching in Sunday schools. First established in the late 18th century by Evangelicals like Hannah More, these schools were very much part of working-class life by the 1820s. Thirty years later they had two million pupils; how much the children learnt it is difficult to judge, but some undoubtedly acquired more knowledge than the schools' founders had intended. Children whose parents could afford 'school-pence' and could spare them from paid employment might attend a dame school or a common day school. With varying success, these small private establishments met a working-class demand for literacy. Autobiographies provide valuable insight into the different ways in which poor children of the early 19th century might gain – to use William Lovett's phrase – 'bread, knowledge and freedom'. [B–D]

Popular though they were, these informal schools were frequently condemned for neglecting 'moral and religious subjects' and producing, in the Duke of Wellington's phrase, 'clever devils'. The churches took the initiative in providing a more centralised and purposeful educational system. The most successful ventures were the British and Foreign Schools Society, set up by the Nonconformist, Joseph Lancaster, in 1808, and the National Society for the Education of the Poor in the Principles of the Established Church, formed by an Anglican clergyman, Andrew Bell, in 1811. As they were financed by voluntary subscription these rival societies could offer poor children a subsidised education, which was cheaper than that provided by the common day schools. [Chapter 3 gives further explanation of Anglicanism and Nonconformity]

The new 'voluntary' schools used the latest teaching method, the monitorial system, by which hundreds of children could be taught in one room by one teacher with the help of monitors. These were older pupils who instructed the younger ones in the lessons they themselves had just learned. They taught the 'three Rs', reading, writing and arithmetic, through the medium of another R – religion. This was Anglican in the 'National' schools and non-denominational in the 'British' schools – to use the shortened names by which they were soon known. These schools proliferated, especially those run by the National Society, which was better funded than its rival and was determined that its Church of England doctrines should dominate in the classroom. The new system made most impact, perhaps, on girls, since voluntary schools saw it as their duty to educate them as well as boys (a view which was seldom shared by educators of the upper and middle classes). It is true that the girls had a curriculum thought to be more suited to their future roles as domestic servants and wives, but teachers often came to regard co-education as beneficial to both sexes. [E–H]

Politicians shared the worries of churchmen about the deficiencies in educational provision, especially in the growing towns where disorder and disaffection might lurk. In 1833 some idealistic Whigs and Radicals, strongly influenced by utilitarian ideas, tried to bring in state-aided compulsory education. But they could only persuade parliament to support school building: the act of 1833 granted £20,000 to religious societies which could raise half the cost themselves. Some MPs had doubts about even this much intervention, though few went so far as Lord Melbourne who remarked that he did not believe in education 'because the Pagets got on so damned well without it'.

In practice the greater part of the grant went to Anglican schools in richer areas. This further strengthened the position of the Church of England, which (like the Nonconformist churches) was anxious to preserve its independent position in the field of education. In 1839 it successfully resisted Whig attempts to change the rules concerning the distribution of the grant and to introduce non-sectarian teacher training – Lord John Russell, the Home Secretary, regarded National schools as 'mummeries of superstition'. But the Anglican Church had to accept the establishment of a government Committee for Education and the appointment of school inspectors. Further state action provoked Nonconformist resistance. In 1843 Dissenters objected so much to a clause in the Conservatives' Factory Bill setting up Anglican-controlled factory schools that the government had to drop it. [I–K]

In spite of such obstruction the Education Committee extended its work, thanks largely to the impassioned efforts of its first Secretary, Sir James Kay-Shuttleworth (formerly J. P. Kay). By the late 1840s (the grant having been increased to £100,000 a year) he had introduced a pupil-teacher scheme, which led indirectly to more government control of schools. In 1851 about one in eight of the population attended a day elementary school, and this was more likely to be a publicly-funded voluntary school than a common day school. Debate now raged about whether the state should extend its educational role. [L–N]

How much good had early 19th-century educators done? The marriage registers show that more men and women were literate by mid-century. [A] Reformers had also hoped for a more biddable and God-fearing populace, though some contemporaries were unhappy about the attempt to mould children's characters. Many historians, too, emphasise this element of social control in Victorian education, whereas others draw attention to its limitations in practice. After all, few working-class children spent more than four years in school and the poorest attended no school at all – many whom Henry Mayhew interviewed in London streets showed little sign of education. Also, many of the unsubsidised, uninspected schools survived into the second half of the century and they did not try so hard to indoctrinate their pupils. Finally, we should not assume that the children were – to use Dickens's phrase – 'little pitchers', whose minds could be filled at will. They were probably influenced less by alien school than by familiar home, neighbourhood and work. [O–Q]

A Percentages of adult males and females unable to sign the marriage register 1839–1912

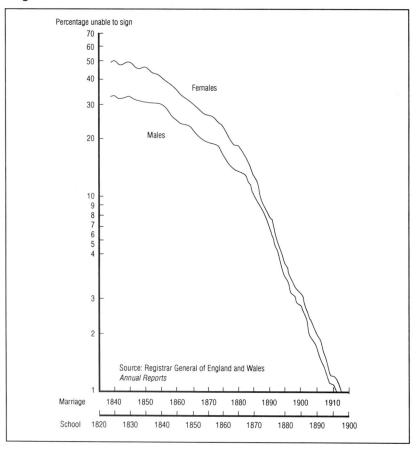

B Hannah More describes her good works in the Mendip area

When I settled in this country thirteen years ago, I found the poor in
many of the villages sunk in a deplorable state of ignorance and vice.
There were, I think, no Sunday schools in the whole district, except one
in my own parish, which had been established by our own respectable
rector, and another in the adjoining parish . . . This drew me to the more
neglected villages, which being distant, made it very laborious . . . My
plan of instruction is extremely simple and limited . . . I allow of no
writing for the poor. My object is not to make fanatics, but to train up the
lower classes in habits of industry and piety. I know of no way of
teaching morals but by teaching principles; and of inculcating Christian
principles without a good knowledge of scripture.

from letters to the Bishop of Bath and Wells and William Wilberforce, 1801

C Contrasting reports on dame schools in two cities
i) Manchester

Occasionally, in some of the more respectable districts, there are still to
be found one or two of the old primitive dame schools, kept by a tidy,
elderly female, whose school has an appearance of neatness and order
which strongly distinguishes it from this class of schools . . . [Most
were] in the most deplorable condition. The greater part of them are
kept by females, but some by old men whose only qualification for this
employment seems to be their unfitness for any other. Many of these
teachers are engaged at the same time in other employments such as
shopkeeping, sewing, washing etc. which renders any regular
instruction among the scholars almost impossible. Indeed neither
parents nor teachers seem to consider this as the principal object in
sending them to these schools, but generally say that they go there to
be taken care of and to be out of the way at home. These schools are
generally found in very dirty unwholesome rooms – frequently in close
damp cellars or old dilapidated garrets.

ii) Birmingham

The physical condition of the Dame Schools of Birmingham is much
more satisfactory than could have been anticipated. None of them are
kept in cellars, very few in garrets or bedrooms, and they are generally
more cleanly and better lighted than schools of the same description in
Manchester or Liverpool.

from Reports by the Statistical Societies of Manchester (1834) and
Birmingham (1838)

D Memories of school from 19th-century autobiographies
i) Samuel Bamford, a Radical born in 1788 near Manchester into a weaver's family

I learned the alphabet from my father at his loom; I afterwards went for a short time to the parish clerk at the Free School, but I learned not anything there; I was not, at that age, quick at imbibing instruction. On Sundays I went with the bigger boys to the Chapel school . . . but neither did I profit by my Sunday education.

Bamford later attended a Methodist Sunday School, where he was taught to write

Big collier lads and their sisters from Siddal Moor were regular in their attendance. From the borders of Whittle, from Bowlee, from the White Moss, from Jumbo and Chadderton and Thornham, came groups of boys and girls with their substantial dinners tied in clean napkins, and the little chapel was so crowded that when the teachers moved they had to wade, as it were, through the close ranked youngsters.

from *Early Days* by S. Bamford (1893)

ii) Joseph Barker, a preacher born in 1806 into a Yorkshire weaver's family

Almost the only opportunity I had of learning anything, except what I might learn at home, was by attending the Sunday-school. When we had work, we had no time to go to school; and when we had not work, we had nothing with which to pay school wages, so that a Sunday-school was the only resource. What little learning, therefore, I did get, I got at home from my brothers and sisters, and at Sunday-school. I recollect my eldest sister and my elder brothers teaching me my letters from a large family Bible that we had, and I also recollect teaching my younger brothers their letters afterwards from the same book.

from *Life, written by himself* by J. Barker (1880)

iii) William Lovett, a Chartist leader born in 1800 to the widow of a sailor in Cornwall

Like most children, when very young, my love of play was far greater than that of learning, for I was sent to all the dame-schools of the village before I could master the alphabet . . . Eventually, however, I was instructed to read by my great-grandmother.

[Lovett was then sent] to a boys' school to learn to write and cipher, thought at that time to be all the education required for poor people. [He made little progress here] where very severe canings were punishments for not recollecting our tasks. [He was then sent to another school]. Here I learned to write tolerably well, and to know a little of arithmetic and the catechism, and this formed the extent of my scholastic requirements.

from *The Life and Struggles of William Lovett* (1876)

E A guide for teachers in monitorial schools gives precise instructions on what to do at all times of the day

Forty-five minutes past nine

The boys would be exercised out to their reading drafts. The following commands would be given by the master or general monitor. 'Hands'; the boys clap on the desks, 'Down', 'Clean', 'Slates'. The writing is then rubbed out. 'Hands', 'Down', 'Look'; the boys then observe the hand of the general monitor, and turn in the direction he moves it in. 'Out'; the boys jump out. 'Front'; they then face the platform. 'Look'; the general monitor turns in the direction of their reading draft stations. 'Go'; they are then led to their drafts by the class monitors, either quite quietly, or repeating their tables.

from *Manual of the System of Primary Instruction, pursued in the Model Schools of the British and Foreign Schools Society* (1831)

F A classroom in a voluntary school

G A model geography lesson about Tyre conducted on the monitorial method

Monitor: Where is it?

Pupil: On an island.

Monitor: Describe the situation of the island.

Pupil: It is at the eastern extremity of the Levant, opposite the northern part of the Holy Land, from which it is separated by a narrow strait.

Monitor: What occasioned its erection on an island?

Pupil: Its being attacked by Nebuchadnezzar.

Monitor: In what tribe was it included?

Pupil: Asshur.

Monitor: For what was it remarkable?

Pupil: Commercial prosperity.

Monitor: In what class of powers should we place it?

Pupil: Naval.

Monitor: Was the second Tyre ever taken?

Pupil: Yes.

Monitor: By whom?

Pupil: Alexander the Great.

Monitor: Cite a passage of Scripture relating to that event.

Pupil: Isaiah xxiii.

from *The Bleak Age* by J. L. & Barbara Hammond (1934)

H A schoolmaster explains his timetable for a National school near Newcastle

The boys and girls work together until the hour for sewing arrives; then a separation takes place, the boys working higher rules in arithmetic than we require of the girls. In our mining district the boys go very early to work, and hence it is necessary that at the same age they should be more advanced than the girls . . . After now having had some experience of the working of Mixed Schools for some time, I have no hesitation in stating, that for the generality of our villages they have some advantages. They are the cheapest, for you can provide a superior master to superintend the mental training, a seamstress being sufficient for the sewing, etc. The manners of the boys are softened by association with the girls, and the girls' minds strengthened by coming into contact with the stronger intellect of the boys. Separate play-grounds will in all instances be required, and the watchful eye of a vigilant and pains-taking teacher.

from a letter by Frederick Wade in the *National Society Monthly Paper* (1851)

I The agricultural riots of 1831 occasioned this article in the *Edinburgh Review*, a periodical which influenced many Whigs

Let no man think that, if the spirit of discontent and outrage should once insinuate itself into the manufacturing districts, it could be suppressed or kept down by force. So mighty a mass cannot be dragooned and coerced into obedience. If we would prolong that security which has been the principal foundation of our prosperity, we must show the labourers that we are interested in their support . . . For this reason, we are deeply impressed with the conviction that Parliament ought to lose no time in setting about the organisation of a really useful system of public education . . . [Thus the poor will be] instructed in the duties and obligations enjoined by religion and morality.

from *Causes and Cure of Disturbances and Pauperism* in *Edinburgh Review* (1831)

J Radical MP, John Roebuck, uses similar arguments to persuade parliament to agree to the principle of universal state education. This would give the people a thorough understanding
of the circumstances on which their happiness depended, and of the powers by which those circumstances were controlled. They would learn what a government could, and what a government could not do to relieve their distresses – they would learn what depended on themselves and what on others . . . We shall have no more unmeaning discontents – no wild and futile schemes of Reform; we shall not have a stack-burning peasantry – a sturdy pauper population – a monopoly-seeking manufacturing class . . . Neither will there be immoral landlords wishing to maintain a dangerous corn monopoly . . . We shall have a people industrious, honest, tolerant and happy.
In reply Sir Robert Peel argues that no such scheme is necessary
It was not quite correct to assert that education in this empire was so very imperfect. He believed that almost every Gentleman who heard him endeavoured, in his own neighbourhood, to diffuse the benefits of education.

from a debate in the House of Commons, July 1833

K William Cobbett (now a Radical MP), objects to the parliamentary grant on surprisingly conservative grounds
He could not consent to take from the people a single farthing in the way of taxes . . . in order to teach the working classes reading and writing . . . Education was the knowledge necessary for the situation in life in which a man was placed. Take two men for instance – suppose one of them to be able to plough, and the other make hurdles and be a good shepherd. If the first man knew how to read as well as plough, and the other man did not know how to read, even then, he should say, that the latter was the better man.

He feared that the main effect would be to
increase the number of schoolmasters and schoolmistresses – that new race of idlers.

from a speech in the House of Commons, 17 August 1833

L Sir James Kay-Shuttleworth is convinced of the urgent need for more state education
A Christian government cannot permit its citizens to be cradled in ignorance; nurtured by bad example in barbarous manners; brought up without faith and without hope; rude and miserable, the support of sedition, the prey of demagogues, the element of popular tumults, the food of the gaol, the convict ship and the gallows. A Christian commonwealth cannot wait till the indigent are in comfort; till the Arabs [urchins] of our great cities are settled and at rest; till the corrupted and ignorant are so far weaned from gross sensual indulgence, as not to waste the school pence of their children on beer, spirits and tobacco. Are not the recklessness of the desperate, the sensuality which is characteristic of a rude material life, the ignorance which no school has corrected, the apathy never disturbed by faith, the dark despair never penetrated by a ray of spiritual hope fruitful sources for School-income? Are the wretched to be denied the remedy for these evils, because of some barren speculation as to the province of the State in Education?

from a paper on Public Education written in 1853

M Edward Baines, a Congregationalist and editor of the *Leeds Mercury*, argues strongly against further government intervention in education. One of his reasons is that it
would reduce the people of this country to a state of pupilage as complete as that of the people of Prussia, or even of China; it would annihilate freedom of education, freedom of the press, freedom of conscience, and freedom of industry.

from an article in *Congregational Magazine* (1843)

N But the Marxist writer, Frederick Engels, considers that the state should do more
The Ministry, with its whole enormous budget of £55,000,000, has only the trifling item of £40,000 for public education, and, but for the fanaticism of the religious sects which does at least as much harm as good, the means of education would be yet more scanty. As it is, the State church manages its national schools and the various sects their sectarian schools for the sole purpose of keeping the children of the brethren of the faith within the congregation, and of winning away a poor childish soul here and there from some other sect . . . [Thus]

sectarian hatred and bigotry are awakened as early as possible, and all rational mental and moral training shamefully neglected. The working-class has repeatedly demanded of Parliament a system of strictly secular public education, leaving religion to the ministers of the sects; but, thus far, no Ministry has been induced to grant it. The minister is the obedient servant of the bourgeoisie.

from *The Condition of the Working Class in England* by F. Engels (1844)

0 Dickens pours scorn on current educational ideas in this passage from *Hard Times*, where Thomas Gradgrind, a wealthy industrialist, visits his model school and interrogates a child from the local circus

'Cecilia Jupe. Let me see. What is your father?'

'He belongs to the horse-riding, if you please, Sir.'

Mr Gradgrind frowned, and waved off the objectionable calling with his hand.

'We don't want to know anything about that, here. Your father breaks horses, don't he?'

'If you please, Sir, when they can get any to break, they do break horses in the ring, Sir.'

'You mustn't tell us about the ring, here. Very well, then. Describe your father as a horsebreaker. He doctors sick horses, I dare say.'

'Oh yes, Sir.'

'Very well, then. He is a veterinary surgeon, a farrier, and horsebreaker. Give me your definition of a horse.'

(Sissy Jupe thrown into the greatest alarm by this demand.)

'Girl number twenty unable to define a horse!' said Mr Gradgrind, for the general behoof of all the little pitchers.

'Girl number twenty possessed of no facts, in reference to one of the commonest of animals! Some boy's definition of a horse. Bitzer, yours.'

. . . .

'Quadruped. Graminivorous. Forty teeth, namely, twenty-four grinders, four eye-teeth, and twelve incisive. Sheds coat in the spring; in marshy countries, sheds hoofs, too. Hoofs hard, but requiring to be shod with iron. Age known by marks in the mouth.' Thus (and much more) Bitzer.

'Now girl number twenty,' said Mr Gradgrind. 'You know what a horse is.'

from *Hard Times* by Charles Dickens (1854)

P The children encountered by Henry Mayhew in the London streets had not often received much education

When quite young the coster-girl is placed out to nurse with some neighbour . . . As soon as the child is old enough to go alone, the court is its play-ground, the gutter its school-room, and under the care of an elder sister the little one passes the day, among children whose mothers like her own are too busy . . . to be able to mind the family at home. When the girl is strong enough, she in turn is made to assist the mother by keeping guard over the younger children, or, if there are none, she is lent out to carry about a baby, and so made to add to the family income by gaining her sixpence weekly. Her time is from the earliest years fully occupied; indeed, her parents cannot afford to keep her without doing and getting something. Very few of the children receive the least education. 'The parents,' I am told, 'never give their minds to learning, for they say,'What's the use of it? that won't earn a gal a living."

Sometimes, though, Mayhew found true dedication to learning. A 15-year-old flower girl, who had been orphaned at the age of eight, told him how she and her brother and sister had acquired some education 'We can all read.' Here the three somewhat insisted upon proving to me their proficiency in reading, and having produced a Roman Catholic book, the 'Garden of Heaven', they read very well. 'I put my brother and sister to a Roman Catholic school – and to Ragged schools – but I could read before mother died. My brother can write, and I pray to God that he'll do well with it.'

from *London Labour and the London Poor* by H. Mayhew (1851)

Q A modern historian argues that reformers were not as important as they thought they were

It was unlikely that anyone looking back on all this would recall school as a pleasant or happy experience. Nonetheless, there was little about school conditions or methods, apart from the physical segregation of the sexes, that conflicted with the treatment which children expected at home or with the attitudes which non-school experience led them to accept as normal. Discipline, adult authority, corporal punishment, discomfort, different gender roles, all these were familiar inside the home . . . School was a significant part of growing up, and an important influence on a child's ideas about the world and how to behave in it. But it was only one strand among many, and for the working-class child with only a short time in school that was likely to end by the age of twelve, it was not the dominant or decisive element; the home and the neighbourhood, and later on the workplace and the pub, had superior influence in shaping the outlook of working-class youths and young adults.

from *The Rise of Respectable Society* by F. M. L. Thompson (1988)

Questions

1 To what extent do the experiences conveyed in sources B, C and D help to explain the 1840 literacy rate shown in source A? **(8 marks)**

2 Andrew Bell compared the monitorial school to a steam engine or a spinning machine. How far is this comparison borne out by sources E–H? **(8 marks)**

3 Using sources I–N, evaluate the arguments for and against state educational provision. **(10 marks)**

4 Select from the sources an example of each of the following views and explain each choice in a sentence: utilitarian; *laissez-faire*; religious; secular. **(4 marks)**

5 How useful are sources O–Q in enabling you to judge the extent to which educational reformers managed to change working-class behaviour? **(10 marks)**

7 CONTROLLING THE WORKPLACE

In 1836 Dr Andrew Ure wrote of the 'blessings of the factory system', in whose 'spacious halls' the 'benignant power of steam summons around him his willing menials'. The following year John Fielden, a cotton manufacturer and Radical MP, described the same system as a 'curse', which allowed avaricious employers 'to exact more labour from their hands [employees] than they were fitted to perform'. These conflicting views sum up the bitter debate about 'manufactories' which raged at this stage of the Industrial Revolution. From the debate a crucial question arose: were workers being so exploited that government intervention was required?

While it had always been the case that men, women and children had worked long hours in dangerous and unhealthy conditions for low wages, it was not until the 19th century that this became a matter for political concern. Factories, although still not the typical workplace in Britain, attracted attention by their very size, by their reliance on the cheap labour of women and children and by the disciplined intensity of work which power-driven machines demanded. Before 1820 several Acts had placed limits on the hours children were allowed to work in textile mills but no inspectors were appointed to enforce the law. [A]

The first supporters of further legislation in the 1830s were Tory landowners, inspired partly by humanitarian concern and partly (historians now argue) by resentment of newly prosperous industrialists. The campaign was initiated by Tory Churchman Richard Oastler, who wrote powerful letters to the *Leeds Mercury* denouncing 'Yorkshire Slavery'. Working men in the industrial communities were inspired by him to set up Short Time Committees to press for a ten-hour working day. In 1832 another Tory, Michael Sadler, introduced a bill aimed at achieving this and chaired a Select Committee on child labour, but he lost his seat in the general election at the end of that year. [B–C]

The more utilitarian Whigs needed to be thoroughly convinced that factory legislation would promote the general good. The shocking details of Sadler's report did not wholly convince them and they appointed a Royal Commission to conduct a further inquiry which would not 'be narrowed to the views of any class, or party or interest'. Its revelations (as well as the speeches of the new Tory champion of factory children, Lord Ashley) were still enough to persuade Parliament to pass the Factory Act of 1833. This forbade the employment in textile mills of children under nine and limited those under 13 and 18 to working eight and twelve hours a day respectively. It also arranged for inspection. But since only four inspectors were appointed for the whole country the act was easily evaded, especially as there were no compulsory birth certificates before 1836. Nevertheless, even the Socialist, Frederick Engels, had to admit in 1842 that 'most of the crying evils [had] disappeared', though the clause requiring children to have two hours' education a day was, as he said, 'a dead letter'. [D–E]

The act did not have any effect on the time worked by adults and thus the Ten Hours Movement continued unabated. A new argument was now introduced: that women as well as children needed legal protection. Different people made the case for different motives. On the one hand, middle-class reformers hoped that limiting the hours of working-class women would improve the deplorable standards of housekeeping, motherhood and morality said to prevail among them. On the other hand, male workers wanted to enhance their own position in the labour market by reducing female competition and to achieve the ten-hour day for themselves 'behind women's petticoats'. The campaign was eventually successful. In 1844 a Factory Act was passed limiting women's work to twelve hours a day and cutting the hours of children to six and a half. Another Factory Act prescribed a maximum ten-hour day for women and young people in 1847 but employers still managed to keep factories open round the clock by the use of a relay system. It was not until the acts of 1850 and 1853, which prevented women and young people from working between 6pm and 6am, that the goal of the Ten Hours Movement was achieved. [F–I]

Meanwhile, the Victorian public had been further horrified by the much-publicised report of the 1842 Commission on the Employment of Children in Mines. Not only did the Commissioners draw attention to the miseries endured by these children, they also exceeded their brief by reporting on the extent of underground labour performed by women in conditions considered to be grossly indecent. So convinced were MPs by the graphic details of the report, with its even more vivid pictures, that there was little opposition to Lord Ashley's bill banning pit labour for all females as well as for boys under 12. When coal-owning MPs introduced an amendment to lower this age limit to 10 Ashley accepted it, 'in order to save the women'. So the Mines Act of 1842 became law. It was hailed as a moral triumph. In fact, as there was only one inspector and no alternative source of female income in the mining areas, hundreds of women continued to work underground – rather than concentrating on their domestic duties as reformers had intended. [J–L]

By 1850 successive governments had intervened to give young and female textile workers and miners the protection which, as 'unfree agents', they were thought to need. Not until the 1860s was legislation extended to other factories and to agricultural field gangs. The conditions of the many women in domestic service and 'sweated' trades like dress-making aroused less moral indignation at this time. Historians suggest that this was because, arduous and ill-paid though such labour was, it seemed to fall within a woman's 'natural sphere'. [M]

Very few would now question the necessity for limiting child labour, though it was probably the advent of compulsory education (in the 1880s) more than the factory acts which really put an end to it. But there is no agreement on how women felt about the laws protecting them. Did they welcome shortened hours as a respite from labour or did they resent the consequent loss of income and freedom? In spite of the efforts of modern scholars, their feelings remain largely hidden from history. [N–O]

A Employment in textile factories in Great Britain, 1839

	Cotton	Worsted	Woollen	Silk	Flax
Number of factories	1,795	416	1,291	268	322
Workforce/factory	142	76	41	128	107
males under 10	1,108	321	869	1,031	152
females under 10	731	417	649	1,461	114
males 10–12	5,963	1,595	2,628	2,343	761
females 10–12	4,475	2,201	2,052	3,769	636
males 13–17	40,610	3,753	10,906	3,185	4,560
females 13–17	55,688	10,129	9,159	8,410	10,197
males over 18	63,495	3,024	18,236	4,304	4,643
females over 18	82,644	10,192	9,050	9,730	13,517
Total workforce	254,714	31,632	53,549	34,233	34,480
Males	111,176	8,693	32,639	10,863	10,116
Females	143,538	22,939	20,910	23,370	24,364
% adult males	24.9%	9.6%	34.0%	12.6%	13.5%

from the Returns of the Factory Inspectorate, 1839

B Richard Oastler uses the imagery of the anti-slavery campaign to convey the miseries of factory work

Thousands of little children, both male and female, but principally female, from seven to fourteen years of age, are daily compelled to labour from six o'clock in the morning to seven in the evening, with only – Britons, blush while you read it! – with only thirty minutes allowed for eating and recreation. Poor infants! ye are indeed sacrificed at the shrine of avarice, without even the solace of the negro slave . . . He knows it is his sordid, mercenary master's interest that he should live, be strong and healthy. Not so with you. Ye are doomed to labour from morning to night for one who cares not how soon your weak and tender frames are stretched to breaking! . . . The blacks may be fairly compared to beasts of burden, kept for their master's use; the whites, to those which others keep and let for hire. If I have succeeded in calling the attention of your readers to the horrid and abominable system on which the worsted mills in and near Bradford is conducted, I have done some good. Why should not children working in them be protected by legislative enactments?

from a letter to the *Leeds Mercury*, 16 October 1830

C Sadler's Committee interviews a workhouse inmate, 23-year-old Elizabeth Bentley, about her work in a flax-mill where, from the age of six, she worked at least 13 hours a day.

Do you consider doffing a laborious employment? – Yes.

Explain what it is you had to do. – When the frames are full, they have to stop the frames, and take the flyers off, and take the full bobbins off, and carry them to the roller; and then put empty ones on, and set the frame going again.

Does that keep you constantly on your feet? – Yes, there are so many frames, and they run so quick.

Your labour is very excessive? – Yes; you have not time for anything.

Suppose you flagged a little, or were too late, what would they do? – Strap us.

Are they in the habit of strapping those who are last in doffing? – Yes.

Constantly? – Yes.

Severely? – Yes.

Is the strap used so as to hurt you excessively? – Yes, it is.

Elizabeth is now asked about the effects of her work in another factory, where she had to drag heavy baskets of flax

You are considerably deformed in your person in consequence of this labour? – Yes, I am.

You are utterly incapable now of any exertion . . . ? – Yes.

State what you think as to the circumstances in which you have been placed during all this time of labour, and what you have considered as to the hardship and cruelty of it.

(The witness was too much affected to answer the question)

from the Report on Child Labour, 1832

D The same witness makes a statement to the Royal Commission in 1833

Doffing is not so very hard work . . . it was the length of time which we had to work which made it so hard; having to run about so long. I do not consider the employment of doffing either laborious or excessive, as mentioned in that book [the previous report], unless continued for such long hours as we worked . . . We were obliged to look sharp to do the work that was to be done; we could not have done it at all times without strapping. Some of them did not like to look so sharp; not always; they would talk to one another instead of minding their work; that I think was a good reason for strapping them; sometimes they strapped them without occasion; that is when the sides were not full; that was from the overlooker being in an ill humour because they had not done what he told them . . . The last four years I have had very bad health; I attribute it to not being strong enough to bear the work that was put upon me when I was young. I now feel myself unfit for any laborious exertion of any kind whatever.

from the Report on Children's Employment, 1833

E Political economist, J.R. McCulloch, is sceptical about both reports
We do not say . . . that the statements and representations . . . have been proved to be wholly destitute of foundation; but we believe that they have been grossly exaggerated. That abuses have existed in some factories is certain; but these have been rare instances; and, speaking generally, factory workpeople, including non-adults, are as healthy and contented as any class of the community obliged to earn their bread in the sweat of their brow . . . Were [children] to be turned out of the factories . . . four-fifths of them would be thrown loose upon the streets, to acquire a taste for idleness, and to be early initiated in the vicious practices prevalent amongst the dregs of the populace, in Manchester, Glasgow, Leeds and other great towns. Whatever may be the state of society in these towns, we hesitate not to say, that it would have been ten times worse but for the factories. They have been the best and most important academies. Besides taking children out of harm's way, they have imbued them with regular, orderly, and industrious habits.

from *Edinburgh Review*, 1835

F Supporters of the Ten Hours Bill, like Chartist Richard Pilling, linked
  that aim with the pursuit of a male family wage
I was not long in the factory until I saw the evil workings of the accursed system – it is a system, which, above all systems, will bring this country to ruin if it is not altered. I read some of the speeches of the late Mr. Sadler, and I have read many letters of that noble king of Yorkshire – Richard Oastler – and very shortly I became an advocate of the Ten Hours' Bill . . .
In 1842 Pilling led a strike against wage cuts, for which he was
prosecuted
Suppose, gentlemen of the jury, you were obliged to subsist on the paltry pittance given to us in the shape of wages, and had a wife and six helpless children . . . how would you feel? Though you were to confine

me to a dungeon I should not submit to it. I have a nervous wife – a good wife – a wife that I love and cherish, and I have done everything that I could in the way of resisting reductions in wages, that I might keep her and my children from the workhouse, for I detest parish relief . . . [Chartism] was always a wage question, and a ten hours bill with me. I have advocated the keeping up of wages for a long time, and I shall do so till the end of my days.

from the trial of Richard Pilling, 1843

G Leonard Horner, the most active of the factory inspectors, is worried about the extent of women's employment

Twelve hours daily work is more than enough for anyone; but however desirable it might be that excessive working should be prevented, there are great difficulties in the way of legislative interference with the labour of adult men. The case, however, is very different as respects women: for not only are they much less free agents, but they are physically incapable of bearing a continuance of work for the same length of time as men, and a deterioration of their health is attended with far more injurious consequences to Society. The substitution of female for male labour, which has increased to so great an extent of late years has the worst consequences for the social condition of the working-classes, by the women being withdrawn from domestic duties; and diminished comforts at home have the most corrupting influence upon the men.

from the Factory Inspectors' Report of 1843

H Lord Ashley expands on this theme while introducing the Factory Bill in 1844

[Female labour] affects . . . all the arrangements and provisions of domestic economy – thrift and management are altogether impossible . . . Everything runs to waste; the house and children are deserted; the wife can do nothing for her husband and family; she can neither cook, wash, repair clothes, or take charge of the infants; all must be paid for out of her scanty earnings, and, after all, most imperfectly done. Dirt, discomfort, ignorance, recklessness, are the portion of such households . . . because the men can discharge at home none of the especial duties that Providence has assigned to the females.

from a speech in the House of Commons, 15 March 1844

I Middle-class opinion tended to support Ashley's view but there were some early feminist writers who drew attention to

the anomalous condition of women in this Christian land of ours. I call it anomalous because it inculcates one thing as the rule of right, and

77

decrees another as the law of necessity. 'Woman's mission', of which people can talk so well, and write so prettily, is incompatible with 'Woman's POSITION', of which no one dares to think, much less to speak. We cry out against unnatural mothers; but the mother must live – to live she must work, and make her children work as soon as they can use their little hands . . . What alternatives do you leave her between this course of unnatural cruelty and absolute starvation? These are the questions to be asked and answered; or our merciful reforms, and educational systems, and ten-hours bills are like to be only new forms of injustice and oppression.

from *Woman's Mission' and Woman's Position* by A. Jameson (1843)

J Girls and women talk about their work to the Mines Commission
Maria Mallender (9): I am a trapper [opener of trap-doors for the trucks to pass through]. I sit in the dark, but they often give me a bit of a candle.
Betty Mallender (11): I don't like being in the pit, but I'm forced. I would rather be at school.
Mary Day (16): If I had anything to do out of the pit, and had good wages, I should like it better.
Hannah Clarkson (16): I like going to the pit, but I would rather go into service. I don't like the confinement, but it does not tire me very much.
Elizabeth Day (17): We have to hurry [pull loaded trucks] in trousers as you saw us today when you were in the pit. Generally I work naked down to the waist like the rest . . . It is very hard work for us all. It is harder work than we ought to do . . . The men behave well to us and never insult or ill-use us.
Ann Eggley (18): We go out at 4 in the morning . . . we get out after 4, sometimes at 5, in the evening. We work the whole time except an hour for dinner, and sometimes we haven't time to eat. The work is far too hard for me . . . Sometimes when we get home at night we have not power to wash and then we go to bed . . . Father said last night it was both a shame and a disgrace for girls to work as we do, but there was nought else for us to do.
Ellspee Thomson (40): I can say to my own cost that the bairns are much neglected when both parents work below; for neighbours, if they keep the children, require as much as the women sometimes earn, and neglect them. The oppression of the coal-bearing is such as to injure women in after-life; and few exist whose legs are not injured, or haunches, before they are 30 years of age. I think colliers' daughters are full as virtuous as other women, only their habits are so different from being taken down so early, especially as collier men think the lasses need less education.

from the Mines Report, 1842

K The report included drawings of the girls to illustrate their work; this one shows a girl 'hurrying'

L One of the commissioners sums up his reactions

Shall it then be said in the very heart of our own country . . . that there shall exist a state of society in which hundreds of young girls are sacrificed to such shameless indecencies, filthy abominations, and cruel slavery as is found to exist in our coal-pits? Chained, belted, harnessed like dogs in a go-cart, – black, saturated with wet, and more than half-naked, – crawling upon their hands and feet, and dragging their heavy loads behind them, – they present an appearance indescribably disgusting.

from the Mines Report, 1842

M Henry Mayhew interviews a typical example of the 'sweated' needlewomen working in London

I was conducted by one who knew the trade well to a hard-working woman living in one of the close foetid [stinking] courts running out of Gray's Inn Lane. Her statement was as follows: 'I make the soldiers' trousers and jackets, and the undress white ones . . . The soldiers' trousers are 6½d a pair. I can make two pair in a day, but it must be a very long day . . . The undress white jackets are 5d each, and they take as much thread as the trousers. I couldn't make two of those in a day . . . They're much harder work than the trousers; then they must be kept so very clean; if we soil them we're made to pay for 'em . . . The soldiers have to pay 8s for their trousers, and 8s for their jackets – so I hears . . . It's not a farthing more than 3s a week that I can earn, take it all the year round; and out of that there's thread, candle, and firing to be taken away . . . leaving about 1s 6d for my clear earnings, after working the whole week through. But that's better than nothing.

from a letter to the *Morning Chronicle*, 13 November 1849

N A historian analyses the motives behind the 'patriarchal' [male-dominated] legislation which protected women
The predominance of women (and children) in the early factories served to accentuate the anxieties of male workers. It also increased their attempts to control women's access to paid employment and the organizations aimed at advancing the conditions and legal rights of wage labourers. Their interest in controlling women's labour coincided with the concern of a growing number of politicians and philanthropists that certain types of labour did not accord with their definition of femininity and standards of morality. Nor did such work concur with their perception of the 'domestic ideal', which by this time they were avidly seeking to establish in their own lives.

from *Women and Industrialization* by Judy Lown (1990)

O But another historian does not think that the patriarchal explanation is entirely appropriate
It has been argued that the male dominated trade unions selfishly sought to impede the employment of women, with whom they felt competitive in the labour market and whom they preferred to retain as dependent domestic workers . . . The strategy was not entirely disadvantageous to working women. To think so is to misunderstand the material conditions of working-class experience . . . Women workers as well as being female are also members of the working class. Class action which tried to raise the price of labour usually had beneficial effects, if not directly on women's wages, then indirectly through increased family wages. This exposes the fallacy that women workers might be subject to disabilities in the guise of protective legislation.

from an article by Jane Humphries (1977)

Questions

1 To what extent does the evidence quoted in source D contradict that quoted in source C? How far does this call into question the methods used in compiling the 1832 Report? **(8 marks)**

2 Compare the usefulness of sources A–E for judging the extent and nature of child labour in the 1830s. **(8 marks)**

3 What light is shed by sources F–I on the lives of working-class women in the early 19th century? **(8 marks)**

4 Why do you think the government decided to ban the female labour shown in sources J, K and L but not that described in source M? **(6 marks)**

5 In the light of sources N and O, and of your own knowledge, how far would you agree that protective legislation for women in the early 19th century was introduced to benefit men? **(10 marks)**

8 SANITISING TOWNS

It was quite common in the 1840s for parliament to suspend its sittings because of the unbearable stench from the Thames. This is not surprising since the river received most of the sewage of London, whose population had increased from 959,000 in 1801 to 1,948,000 in 1841. What is perhaps surprising is that health problems, like those caused by the state of the Thames, occupied much less parliamentary time in the first half of the 19th century than religious questions such as the proper use of Church revenue.

Every decade towns grew more rapidly, as young men and women travelled to them in search of better paid work and more independence. London's growth was outstanding but industrial cities, ports, spas and seaside resorts all increased substantially in size. Thus by 1851 more than half the British people lived in towns. The trend aroused much comment. Many writers blamed urbanisation for all the problems of the day: crime, disease, ignorance, irreligion, political disorder and class conflict. Some of these pessimists longed nostalgically for an old rural society, where the upper classes were responsible and the lower classes were subservient; others demanded cures to remediable ills. More optimistic commentators extolled the prosperity generated by the growing cities and saw in them opportunities for more political and religious liberty. [A–F]

Towns attracted the attention of parliament because of their growing social problems and political awareness. The arrival in Britain of Asiatic cholera, which killed over 30,000 people in 1831–2, caused much alarm. Although the link between cholera and polluted water was not yet known, some doctors (like J. P. Kay) saw its connection with urban squalor; MPs were more concerned about it as a cause of town riots during the Reform crisis [Chapter 2]. After the reform agitation had died down, further urban pressure groups like the anti-Poor Law Movement, the Ten Hours Movement, the Chartists and the Anti-Corn Law League alarmed Westminster during the 1830s and 1840s. Increasingly, political economists urged legislation to halt the decline of religion and morality in towns. They helped to inspire the ecclesiastical and educational reforms discussed in Chapters 3 and 6. [G–H]

The first specifically urban reform was the Municipal Corporations Act of 1835. Radical MP Joseph Parkes described it as 'the steam engine for the mill built by Parliamentary Reform'. The Act got rid of the ancient corporations of 178 boroughs and put elected bodies in their place. Although the franchise turned out to be narrower than promised, most ratepaying businessmen, shopkeepers and artisans gained the vote; they generally used it, as the Whigs had intended, to oust the Tories. Over the next few years more towns were granted new-style corporations, whose powers were mainly to do with creating police forces and ensuring public order. Some corporations acquired wider environmental powers by means of expensive local Improvement Acts. But although there was much talk about providing sewers, water supplies, smoke control, public parks and street cleaning, little was achieved. [I–J]

By the late 1830s, parliament received more information on urban problems from Factory Inspectors and Poor Law Commissioners. It was a report from the latter which inspired the House of Lords in 1838 to set up an Inquiry into the Sanitary Conditions of the Labouring Classes. Edwin Chadwick, who had already served on the Factory and Poor Law Inquiries, was put in charge of it. He did most of the work and in 1842 produced a report so radical that the other Commissioners would not sign it.

It gave a painfully vivid picture of men, women and children living in overcrowded lodging-houses, damp cellars and unventilated back-to-back houses. In streets, yards and courts their refuse accumulated in stinking piles. They collected polluted water from pumps, rivers, ponds and wells. They hung out washing across narrow, smoke-laden streets. Chadwick made explicit the link between insanitary conditions and dangerous diseases like typhus, typhoid, tuberculosis and chronic diarrhoea, endemic in working-class areas. Whereas earlier he had blamed poverty on idleness, here he attributed destitution to the frequent illness or premature death of wage-earners. His main recommendations were that sewage be removed not by 'hand labour' but by suspension in water in glazed, circular drains, and that clean water be supplied by local authorities 'for the common benefit of a town without the agency of private companies'. He suggested that so much government interference and public expense would be justified by the moral as well as the physical improvement of the labouring classes. [K]

Though it received much attention among journalists and novelists, the Sanitary Report made little immediate impact on parliament. In 1843 Peel appointed a Royal Commission to investigate the Health of Towns, which in its reports of 1844 and 1845 confirmed Chadwick's findings and recommended extensive reform. But the Corn Law crisis prevented a Public Health Bill from being introduced until 1847 – after Peel's resignation. Vociferous opposition to this 'un-English' centralisation caused the Whigs to drop the Bill. But in 1848 the approach of a further wave of cholera from Europe induced a greater sense of urgency and the Public Health Bill (the 'Poor Man's Bill') was passed.

The Act established a General Board of Health to supervise local Boards of Health; these were to be set up at the request of one tenth of the inhabitants or when the death rate exceeded 23 per 1,000. The Boards could (but did not have to) provide street cleaning and paving, sewerage systems and water supply. Due to the pressure of local interests, London and Scotland were excluded from the Act. This essentially permissive legislation did not have dramatic results. Some towns began, or continued, to tackle their almost overwhelming sanitary problems. But the opposition of ratepayers, the strength of vested interests (for example, private water companies) and lack of technical expertise meant that progress was slow. Nevertheless, a start had been made. Although that generation of town-dwellers could not expect to live beyond their forties, its children could expect to live into their fifties and its grandchildren into their sixties. [L–P]

A These figures (shown in thousands) illustrate the rapid growth of towns in the first half of the 19th century

	1801	1831	1851
Birmingham	71	144	233
Bradford	13	44	104
Derby	11	24	41
Huddersfield	7	19	31
Leeds	53	123	172
Liverpool	82	202	376
Manchester	75	182	303
Nottingham	29	50	57
Oldham	12	32	53
Portsmouth	33	50	72
Sheffield	46	92	135
Wolverhampton	13	25	50

from *A Social History of Housing* by J.Burnett (1978)

B In his early history of the cotton industry, Richard Guest welcomes the new urban age

The progress of the cotton manufacture introduced great changes in the manners and habits of the people [of Lancashire]. The operative workmen being thrown together in great numbers, had their faculties sharpened and improved by constant communication. Conversation wandered over a number of topics not before essayed; the questions of peace and war, which interested them importantly, inasmuch as they might produce a rise or fall of wages, became highly interesting, and this brought them into the vast field of politics and discussions on the character of their Government, and the men who composed it . . . From being only a few degrees above the cattle in the scale of intellect, they became Political Citizens.

from *A History of the Cotton Industry* by R. Guest (1823)

C Tory writer, Robert Southey, finds dangers lurking in the towns
You have a great and increasing population, exposed at all times by the fluctuations of trade to suffer the greatest privations in the midst of a rich and luxurious society, under little or no restraint from religious principle, and if not absolutely disaffected to the institutions of the country, certainly not attached to them: a class of men aware of their numbers and of their strength; experienced in all the details of combination; improvident when they are in receipt of good wages, yet feeling themselves injured when those wages, during some failure of demand, are so lowered as no longer to afford the means of comfortable subsistence; and directing against the country their resentment and indignation for the evils which have been brought upon them by competition and the spirit of rivalry in trade. They have among them intelligent heads and daring minds; and you have already seen how perilously they may be wrought upon by seditious journalists and seditious orators in times of distress.

from *Sir Thomas More: or, Colloquies on the Progress and Prospects of Society* by R. Southey (1829)

D Whig politician, Henry Brougham, plays on civic pride during a
  successful election speech in Leeds
We don't now live in the days of Barons, thank God – we live in the days of Leeds, of Bradford, of Halifax, and of Huddersfield – we live in the days when men are industrious and desire to be free; and not when they are lazy and indolent, and deserve to be trampled upon and dominated over; therefore you are bound to have your rights, and to choose your representatives.

from *Leeds Mercury*, 27 July 1830

E J. P. Kay's description of working-class conditions in Manchester has
  already been quoted [Chapter 1, source C]. In this extract he
  recommends political action to remedy them
That these evils should have been overlooked by the aristocracy of the country, cannot excite surprise. Very few of their order reside in, or near our large provincial towns . . . Their parks are not often traversed by those capable of being the exponents of the evils endured by the working classes of large towns, and the hoarse voice of popular discontent disturbs not the Arcadian [Paradise-like] stillness of the scene . . . What wonder then, that the miseries of the people have been solemnly denied in both houses of Parliament – that popular tumults have been attributed . . . to the instigation of unprincipled leaders? . . . The public welfare will be most powerfully promoted by every event which exposes the condition of the people to the gentry of England.

from *The Moral and Physical Condition of the Working Classes* by J. P. Kay (1832)

F Some of the cheap broadsides sold in the streets of industrial towns give a more cheerful impression of urban life

In Oldham streets at dinner time
  The workfolk how they flock,
Just as you hear the church clock chime
  Each day at half-past twelve o'clock.
In such a hurry crowds you meet
At the turn of every street;
You'd think all the world, as I'm a sinner,
Wur come to Oldham o' getting their dinner. . . .
There's Jones', Bell's. and Castle Mill,
  Gleadhill's and Hillon's send out their ranks;
Till half-past one they're never still –
  It's like the fair at Lousey Banks.
The lasses then, who think they're fair,
Blackball their heels and curl their hair,
Sayin', 'Put up my hair nicely Nelly,
For today at noon I'st meet my felly.'

from *Oldham Streets at Dinner Time*, a broadside ballad.

G The Revd Vaughan Thomas gives the citizens of Oxford advice on how to avoid cholera

Filthiness, foul smells, and all lodgements of nastiness in Houses, Courts, Alleys, and especially in confined situations, tend to produce Disease. If you wish to preserve your own health, or the healthiness of your city, be cleanly in your persons and premises. Do not let any sort of filth gather in drains and gutters, especially when they run through narrow courts, and in the midst of a thickly-peopled neighbourhood. If the pump be handy, clean out your gutters, morning and evening, by pumping; if the pump be not handy, throw down buckets of water. Nothing is more likely to spread Disease than the foul smells coming off from stagnations of filth.

from *Memorials of the Malignant Cholera in Oxford* (1835)

H This pamphlet gives different advice

Ought we not to view the late fatal disease, which made such havoc amongst us, carrying away our friends and neighbours so rapidly, as a direct visitation of the Almighty? Should we not enquire whether the design of the Lord has been answered? Are we more obedient and thankful people? We ought to feel grateful to God, who in the midst of death preserved us alive . . . Oh! Let each of us ever consider the salvation of our souls, the one thing needful.

from a leaflet sold in the Midlands, 1832

**I Richard Cobden (later one of the leaders of the Anti-Corn Law
League) extols the benefits for Manchester of the Municipal
Corporations Act, 'a charter of popular self-government'**

Every man's vote, however humble his circumstances may be, is of
equal value with his wealthiest neighbour's . . . The banker or the
merchant, though worth a million, and though he ride in his carriage to
the polling booth, can only record the same number of votes as the poor
artisan, who walks there perhaps slip-shod or aproned from his garret
or cellar.

from *Incorporate Your Borough* by A Radical Reformer (1837)

**J The City of Oxford had many Boards of Improvement Commissioners
in the 1830s and 1840s. But replies to an inquiry in 1848 do not
suggest that much real improvement had taken place**

Have the authorities of the town suggested spontaneously the adoption
of complete sanitary arrangements of any one kind; for example,
complete house drainage with sewerage and with suburban drainage?
Neither; and the greatest unwillingness exists in the Board of
Commissioners to be driven into expenses for sanitary purposes.
Have the authorities of the town done anything to obtain an abundant
and economical supply of water . . . ?
The water supplied by the Corporation is intermittent and very deficient.
[The pumps] are in the lowest level of the city, and at the tail of nearly all
the sewers! . . . Out of 4,500, only 160 take the water, caused by the
irregular and deficient supply, and the high price charged for it.
Have the authorities of the town made any exertions to obtain a
combination of these works – that is, the water supply with the
sewerage, the house drainage, the street cleaning, and the protection of
property and life from fire?
Never; and not likely to do so, until compelled by Parliamentary
interposition.

from *Oxford Herald*, 29 July 1848

**K Brief extracts from Chadwick's Report give some impression of the
whole**

Dr Duncan reports on Liverpool: There is beneath the dayroom a cellar,
let off either by the landlord or tenant of the house, to a more
improvident class of labourers: which cellar, in almost all cases, is small
and damp, and often crowded with inhabitants to excess. These cellars
are . . . the source of many diseases, particularly catarrh, rheumatic
affections, and . . . typhus.
Dr Howard reports on Manchester: Whole streets in these quarters
are unpaved and without drains or main-sewers, are worn into deep
ruts and holes, in which water constantly stagnates, and are so covered

with refuse and excrement as to be almost impassable from depth of mud, and intolerable from stench.

Mr Baker reports on Leeds: In one *cul-de-sac* . . . there are 34 houses, and in ordinary times, there dwell in these houses 340 persons . . . but as these houses are many of them receiving houses for itinerant labourers . . . at least twice that number are [sometimes] congregated. The name of this place is the Boot and Shoe Yard, in Kirkgate, a location from whence the Commissioners removed, in the days of the cholera, 75 cart-loads of manure, which had been untouched for years, and where there now exists a surface of human excrement of very considerable extent, to which these impure and unventilated dwellings are additionally exposed. The property is said to pay the best annual interest of any cottage property in the borough.

Mr Wood of Manchester contrasts the expectation of life in town and countryside

	Average Age of Death	
	In Manchester	In Rutlandshire
Professional persons and gentry	38	52
Tradesmen, farmers and graziers	20	41
Mechanics and labourers	17	38

Chadwick understands that the ethos of self-help (as advocated in the Poor Law Report) is not always useful

The individual labourer has little or no power over the internal structure and economy of the dwelling which has fallen to his lot. If the water be not laid on in the other houses in the street, or if it be unprovided with proper receptacles for refuse, it is not in the power of any individual workman . . . to procure them. He has as little control over the external economy of his residence as of the structure of the street before it, whether it shall be paved or unpaved, drained or undrained. It may be said that he might cleanse the street before his own door. By some local acts the obligation to do so is imposed on the individual inhabitants. By those inhabitants who have servants this duty may be and is performed, but the labourer has no servant; all of his family who are capable of labour are out a-field, or in the manufactory or the workshop, at daybreak, and return only at nightfall, and this regulation is unavoidably neglected.

from *Report on the Sanitary Condition of the Labouring Population of Great Britain* by Edwin Chadwick (1842)

L Thomas Carlyle advocates legislation

The Legislature, even as it now is, could order all dingy Manufacturing Towns to cease from their soot and darkness; to let in the blessed sunlight, the blue of Heaven, and become clear and clean . . . Baths, free air, a wholesome temperature, ceilings twenty feet high, might be

ordained, by Act of Parliament, in all establishments licensed as Mills
. . . Every toiling Manchester, its smoke and soot all burnt, ought it not,
among so many world-wide conquests, to have a hundred acres or so of
greenfield, with trees on it, conquered, for its little children to disport in;
for its all-conquering workers to take a breath of twilight air in? . . . And
to whatever 'vested interest', or suchlike, stood up, gainsaying merely,
'I shall lose profits,' – the willing Legislature would answer, 'Yes, but my
sons and daughters will gain health and life, and a soul.'

from *Past and Present* by T. Carlyle (1843)

**M Elizabeth Gaskell's *Mary Barton* was recommended by *Fraser's
Magazine* as a book which answered questions of the kind Carlyle
asked. In this passage two working men go to visit a friend who is
'down with the fever'**
Berry Street was unpaved; and down the middle a gutter forced its way,
every now and then forming pools in the holes with which the street
abounded . . . As they passed, women from their doors tossed
household slops of every description into the gutter; they ran into the
next pool, which overflowed and stagnated . . . You went down one step
even from the foul area into the cellar in which a family of human
beings lived . . . After the account I have given of the state of the street,
no one can be surprised that on going into the cellar inhabited by
Davenport, the smell was so foetid as almost to knock the two men
down. Quickly recovering themselves . . . they began to penetrate the
thick darkness of the place, and to see three or four little children rolling
on the damp, nay wet, brick floor, through which the stagnant, filthy
moisture of the street oozed up; the fireplace was empty and black; the
wife sat on her husband's chair, and cried in the dank loneliness . . . The
'fever' was (as it usually is in Manchester), of a low, putrid, typhoid kind;
brought on by miserable living, filthy neighbourhood. and general
depression of mind and body.

from *Mary Barton* by E. Gaskell (1848)

**N Historian Asa Briggs argues that pessimistic writers like Carlyle, Mrs
Gaskell, Disraeli and Engels**
underestimated the significance of the changes in local government
which gave Manchester its first borough council in 1838. They ignored
many of the manifestations of increasing interest in local reform which
led the Manchester Improvement Committee in 1844 . . . to describe 'the
health and comfort of the working classes' in the worst area of
Manchester as 'a subject of vital importance . . . engrossing much of the
attention, not only of scientific men, but also of the legislature of the
country, and indeed of all classes of society'. By means of such
measures as the Borough Police Act of 1844 and the Sanitary

Improvement Act of 1845, Manchester was drafting, however inadequately, a local sanitary code 'and was giving a lead to most of the other large towns in the country' . . . The social critics of the 1840s ignored the significance of this local legislation as they ignored . . . the significance of Peel's reforms in national government during the same period.

from *Victorian Cities* by A. Briggs (1963)

O **In his study of mid-century Leeds, Brian Barber says that 'there was little real improvement in public health before the last quarter of the nineteenth century'**
[In Leeds] the mortality rate failed to fall before the mid-1870s . . . The

DIPHTHERIA.   SCROFULA.   CHOLERA.

FATHER THAMES INTRODUCING HIS OFFSPRING TO THE FAIR CITY OF LONDON.
(A Design for a Fresco in the New Houses of Parliament.)

P A Punch cartoon of 1858 comments on what public health reforms had achieved by that time

recurring inefficiency of public cleansing . . . continued for 30 years . . . The sewerage system had little impact upon sanitary conditions until the 1880s, when the number of water closets in use began to increase considerably. Undoubtedly, the council's spirited defence of the privy-and-ashpit system did nothing to hasten the change. In many respects Leeds, with its privies, its dilatory record of sewage disposal, and its epidemic victims lying under canvas was not unique, but simply presents an exaggeration of the worst features to be found in other towns. Under such circumstances, it is not at all difficult to appreciate why the aims of the public health propagandists of the 1840s took so long to achieve.

from *Municipal Reform and the Industrial City* ed D. Fraser (1982)

Questions

1 What attitudes to the social trend shown in source A are displayed by the writers of sources B–F? **(10 marks)**

2 Examine the assumptions behind the advice given in sources G and H. **(6 marks)**

3 What do sources I and J tell you about the theory compared with the practice of Municipal Reform? **(6 marks)**

4 F. M. L. Thompson writes that sources like K, L and M only describe 'the conditions of the poorest, most unfortunate, or most disreputable sections of the working classes'. To what extent does this make them less valuable? **(8 marks)**

5 Use sources N–P, and your own knowledge, to comment on the progress made in public health reform during the first half of the 19th century. **(10 marks)**

9 FREEING TRADE

Like the European Common Market in recent years, the 19th-century free trade issue provoked much passion but evoked little comprehension among the general public. Both these complex economic matters have made and broken political reputations, created divisions within parties and filled newspaper columns.

Free traders opposed the old system of protection by which British agriculture and industry were shielded from foreign competition through import duties [tariffs], quotas, prohibitions and special regulations like the Navigation Laws, which insisted on a high proportion of trade being carried out in British ships. A further trade restriction was the new Corn Law, passed in 1815 to protect corn producers: no corn could be imported into the country until the price of English corn reached 80 shillings a quarter. There was always bitter opposition to this 'bread-tax'. [A–B]

The classic case for free trade had been made in the late 18th century by Adam Smith, whose works were frequently re-issued. In *The Wealth of Nations* he argued, with the optimism of his day, that if all countries produced what they were best at producing and traded freely with each other, all would benefit. As Britain's industrial superiority grew, her economists were increasingly struck by the advantages of free trade. It would provide cheaper imports of raw materials and open up export markets, without exposing Britain to much competition. Despite initial caution, the commercial middle classes and urban working classes came to espouse free trade during the first half of the 19th century. However, the politically influential landowning class, which felt threatened by imports of cheap food, continued to advocate protection. Governments tried to strike a balance between these varying viewpoints. [C–D]

In the 1820s Tory Prime Minister Lord Liverpool felt able to pursue a policy of moderate free trade. The new President of the Board of Trade, William Huskisson, was responsible for relaxing the Navigation Laws. He also allowed for reciprocal trade agreements with other countries, introduced a sliding scale of duties for corn and reduced certain other tariffs. He would have taken the policies further but for the strength of Tory protectionist opinion. Another constraint was the government's dependence on customs duties for revenue, since MPs of both parties had combined to defeat an earlier proposal to retain war-time income tax. [E]

The 1830s was not a fruitful time for free trade. Huskisson, who might have joined the Whig cabinet along with other liberal Tories, was killed by a train at the opening of the Liverpool-Manchester railway in 1830. Lord Althorp's 1831 budget sought to reduce duties on a wide range of goods and to make up the revenue by a new tax on property. But it was emasculated by Whig and Tory amendments. So what would have been a significant measure of tariff reform was lost and Whig economic policy is now usually dismissed as indecisive and inexpert. A mounting deficit, for which the Whigs could find no remedy, led to their fall from power in 1841. Just before that Russell had proposed a moderate corn duty to replace the sliding scale. This abortive plan was hailed as a partial triumph for the Anti-Corn Law League, the Manchester pressure group which had been campaigning vigorously for repeal since 1838. One of their main aims was to convert Sir Robert Peel once he became Conservative Prime Minister.

Doubtless Peel had already been influenced by the highly partisan Report of the Import Duties Committee in 1840. Faced with a worsening trade depression, he became convinced that the way to stimulate the economy was to increase demand at home and abroad by reducing duties on many articles; he was also determined to re-introduce income tax. He implemented both policies in the budget of 1842 and lowered duties on corn by introducing a more lenient sliding scale. Although there was protectionist opposition in the party, the policies were popular in the country. By 1845 they were working so well that Peel felt able to bring in a further round of tariff reductions and to renew income tax. But the deteriorating relations between the Prime Minister and his party were revealed in the row over the lower duty proposed on foreign sugar. Opposition came from both West Indian plantation owners and anti-slavery humanitarians, who argued that the measure would encourage the import of foreign sugar produced by slaves rather than sugar from British colonies, where slavery had been abolished in 1833. Their amendment striking out the lower sugar duty passed through parliament but a second vote cancelled it after Peel had threatened to resign. [F–G]

During the debate on the 1845 budget Peel acknowledged several other 'causes combining to increase the prosperity of the country'. Among them was the construction of the railway system which had doubled in size since he came to power, 'rendering travelling more easy and traffic less expensive'. The 1844 Railways Act drawn up by William Gladstone (who was President of the Board of Trade) helped to make this exciting new form of transport available to all classes, by requiring trains to carry third class passengers for a penny a mile. But in spite of advice from some quarters, there was no further attempt to exert any control over this hectic 'railway mania', which left many investors bankrupt and many cities devastated. Historians today suggest that the state got a poorly planned rail network because it refused to take a directing role and clung to *laissez-faire* policies. [H and Q]

Peel's mind was on other matters. Well before the failure of the Irish potato crop and the consequen'famine of 1845, he had decided that duties on corn were harmful to the economy. The League's efficient propaganda and the parliamentary speeches of its leader, Richard Cobden, had helped to bring about this change of mind. Thinking it politically impossible to continue taxing food in a time of famine, Peel decided that the repeal of the Corn Laws could not wait until the Conservative party was ready for it. Unable to persuade his cabinet of this view he resigned in December 1845. Although Russell had already announced the Whigs' conversion to repeal, he was not willing to form a minority government and Peel returned. Corn duties were phased out as part of a free trade package passed through parliament by a combination of Whig and Tory votes in June 1846. Protectionist opposition to repeal, effectively marshalled by Benjamin Disraeli and Lord George Bentinck, was strong enough to split the Conservative party and, once Whig support was withdrawn, the fall of the government was inevitable. Peel's resignation speech referred to the 'abundant and untaxed food' which the labouring classes could now enjoy; in practice, though, repeal did not make bread much cheaper (or ruin farmers) during the next few decades. But it almost certainly helped Britain's trade to expand. [I–N]

In the course of this political drama Peel became a popular hero. He was worshipped even more fervently after his death following a riding accident in 1850. [O–P] The question of whether he deserved the devotion of the working classes is discussed in the specimen essay. [Chapter 11]

A An MP states the protectionist case during the debate on the Corn Law in 1815

Nothing could be more obvious than that the reduction of the price of corn . . . was attributable to the importation of foreign grain. He did not wish the farmers to have a very high price for their corn, but he wished them to have such a price as would protect them in their labours; and if he wished plenty to the poor, he certainly did not wish to see them fed with French corn, or clothed with foreign manufactures. He wished everything to be English, and for this reason he would protect the agriculturalist as well as the manufacturer.

from a speech by Mr Thompson in the House of Commons, 3 March 1815

B The new Corn Law was unpopular from the beginning, as is shown in this declaration made at a Radical meeting in Manchester

The conduct of the late Parliament in passing the Corn Bill, which was obtained under false pretensions and passed at the point of the bayonet, in defiance of the united groans and supplications of the People, was oppressive in its design and cruel in its operation; being neither more nor less than a vile conspiracy between the great Landholders and the Ministers, to extort from the industrious labourer and mechanic, through the very bread they eat, an immense portion of

Taxes for the support of the Borough system, and to enrich themselves
and their pensioned minions, by the sweat of the poor man's brow.

from *Manchester Observer*, 23 January 1819

C Economist Adam Smith makes a rational case against protection
The natural advantages which one country has over another in
producing particular commodities are sometimes so great, that it is
acknowledged by all the world to be in vain to struggle with them. By
means of glasses, hotbeds, and hotwalls, very good grapes can be
raised in Scotland, and very good wine too can be made of them at
about thirty times the expense for which at least equally good wine can
be brought from foreign countries. Would it be a reasonable law to
prohibit the importation of all foreign wines, merely to encourage the
making of claret and burgundy in Scotland? . . . Whether the
advantages which one country has over another, be natural or acquired,
is in this respect of no consequence. As long as the one country has
those advantages, and the other wants them, it will always be
advantageous for the latter . . . to buy from the former than to make.

from *The Wealth of Nations* by Adam Smith (1828 edn.)

**D A petition from City of London businessmen (actually written by
Thomas Tooke as a piece of free trade propaganda) urges**
That freedom from restraint is calculated to give the utmost extension
to foreign trade, and the best direction to the capital and industry of the
country.

That the maxim of buying in the cheapest market, and selling in the
dearest, which regulates every merchant in his individual dealings, is
strictly applicable as the best rule for the trade of the whole nation.

That a policy founded on these principles would render the
commerce of the world an interchange of mutual advantages, and
diffuse an increase of wealth and enjoyments among the inhabitants of
each State.

from Petition of the London Merchants, 1820

**E A popular poem mourns the tragic death of Huskisson, whose free
trade policies were obviously thought to be beneficial to the people**
O Huskisson! O Huskisson!
O Huskisson, in vain our friend!
Why hast thou left thy work undone?
Of good begun is this the end?
. . . . .
Thou should'st have lived, if with thee dies
The poor man's hope of better days.

95

Time stops to weep, but yet shall rise
The sun whose beams shall write thy praise.

from *Elegy* in *Corn Law Rhymes* by Ebenezer Elliott (1831)

F The Select Committee on Import Duties, chaired by Joseph Hume, a Radical MP committed to free trade, adds its weight to the case against protection

On articles of food alone, it is averred, according to the testimony laid before the Committee, that the amount taken from the consumer exceeds the amount of all the other taxes which are levied by the Government. And the witnesses concur in the opinion that the sacrifices of the community are not confined to the loss of revenue, but that they are accompanied by injurious effects upon wages and capital; they diminish greatly the productive powers of the country, and limit our active trading relations . . . Your Committee are persuaded that by imposts on a small number of those articles which are now most productive . . . no loss would occur to the revenue, but, on the contrary, a considerable augmentation might be confidently anticipated.

John McGregor, a secretary in the Board of Trade, is questioned about the sugar duty

Does it bear proportion to the means of our population which it ought to do? – Certainly not. Not only would the consumption of sugar be much greater, but the consumption of tea and coffee, and other things, which come in as auxiliaries in the way of food, would increase.

Has not the consumption of tea and coffee lately extended itself among the middling and poorer classes as a substitute for spirituous liquors? – Yes.

And therefore, as sugar is a necessary accompaniment to that, is it not, in a moral point of view, very important? – Yes.

from the Report on Import Duties, 1840

G Peel seeks to persuade property-owners that it is their public duty to pay income-tax

I am now addressing you after the duration of peace for twenty-five years. I am now exhibiting to you the financial difficulties and embarrassments in which you are placed; and my confident hope and belief is, that following the example of those who preceded you, you will look these difficulties in the face, and not refuse to make similar sacrifices to those which your fathers made for the purpose of upholding the public credit. You will bear in mind that this is no casual and occasional difficulty. You will bear in mind that there are indications amongst all the upper classes of society of increased comfort and enjoyment – of increased prosperity and wealth, and that concurrently with these indications there exists a mighty evil [the deficit] which has been growing up for the last seven years, and which you are now called upon to meet. If you have, as I believe you have, the fortitude and constancy of which you have been set the example, you will not consent with folded arms to view the annual growth of this mighty evil.

from Peel's budget speech in the House of Commons, 11 March 1842

H In a portrait of mid-century England, William Johnston gives only partial approval to Peel's economic policies
The affairs of the nation, and especially financial affairs, which had worn a very gloomy aspect during the latter years of the Melbourne administration, brightened in a wonderful manner under the Peel government. Confidence revived; money became abundant; funds were easily raised in credit; and in 1844 there arose a fever of speculation in railway undertakings which proceeded gradually to a kind of universal madness, which was at its height in the summer of 1845. This madness the successful minister did nothing to check . . . No tongue can tell – no pen describe – the privation and misery which have resulted from the loss of inherited property or hard-earned savings invested in these undertakings, to the excess of which the minister of 1845 lent such fatal encouragement . . .

WORKING MEN!
You Pay a Tax of Tenpence
Upon every Stone of Flour you and your wives and little ones consume.

If there was not the Infamous CORN LAW you and your Families might buy THREE LOAVES for the same money that you now pay for Two.

Upon every Shilling you spend for Bread, Meat, Bacon, Eggs, Vegetables, &c., you pay 4d. Tax for Monopoly.

DOWN, DOWN
WITH THE
Infamous Bread Tax!

I A typical Anti-Corn Law League handbill

It must however be confessed that, but for this madness, which has affected almost every second person in the middle-class community with a sense of loss . . . the country would not at this day have possessed the widely-extended advantages – if, upon the whole they are advantages – of railway communication which it does possess.

from *England As It Is* by W. Johnston (1851)

J Richard Cobden appeals to humanitarian 'members on the other side of the House', among whom he singles out Lord Ashley, to support an anti-Corn Law resolution

I, therefore, exhort the advocates of religion, the advocates of education, the friends of moral and physical improvement, to reflect upon the votes which they are about to give . . . I call upon them to separate themselves from those with whom they are accustomed to act, unless they are prepared to lose all the influence which they have laboured so hard to acquire in the manufacturing districts. I call upon them to support the present measure if they hope to be useful. There are 7,000,000 or 8,000,000 of people without wheaten bread. If the people continue to descend in the scale of physical comfort, and to eat potatoes, the hope of moral improvement which the friends of humanity indulge, must be altogether disappointed.

from a speech in the House of Commons, 15 May 1843

K Lord John Russell changes his mind on the Corn Laws

I used to be of opinion that corn was an exception to the general rules of political economy; but observation and experience have convinced me that we ought to abstain from all interference with the supply of food . . . Let us, then, unite to put an end to a system which has been proved to be the blight of commerce, the bane of agriculture, the source of bitter divisions among the classes, the cause of penury, fever, mortality, and crime among the people.

from a letter to his constituents, 22 November 1845

L In the last of his five long speeches on the Corn Laws, Peel explains why he thinks repeal is necessary

I do not rest my support of this bill merely upon the temporary ground of scarcity in Ireland . . . but I believe that scarcity left us with no alternative but to undertake the consideration of this question; and that consideration being necessary, I think the permanent adjustment of the question is . . . the best policy for all concerned . . . Now, all of you admit that the real question at issue is the improvement of the social and moral condition of the masses of the population; we wish to elevate in the gradation of society that great class which gains its support by manual labour – that is agreed on all hands. The mere interests of the landlords – the mere interests of the occupying tenants, important as they are, are subordinate to the great question – what is calculated to increase the comforts, to improve the condition, and elevate the social character of the millions who subsist by manual labour, whether they are engaged in manufactures or in agriculture . . . I wish to convince them that our object has been so to apportion taxation, that we relieve industry and labour from any undue burden, and transfer it, so far as is consistent with the public good, to those who are better enabled to bear it.

from a speech in the House of Commons, 15 May 1846

M Members of the House of Lords dissent from Repeal
Because it will greatly increase the dependence of this country upon foreign countries for its supply of food, and will thereby expose it to dangers against which former statesmen have thought it essential to take legislative precautions.
Because it is unjust to withdraw protection from the landed interest of this country, while that interest remains subject to exclusive burdens imposed for the purpose of general . . . advantage.
Because the loss to be sustained by the repeal of the Corn Laws will fall most heavily upon the least wealthy portion of the landed proprietors, will press immediately and severely on the tenant-farmers, and through them, with ruinous consequences, on the agricultural labourers.

from a protest in the House of Lords, 25 June 1846

N Average prices of wheat

1820–29	59s. 10d.	(£2.99)
1830–39	56s. 9d.	(£2.84)
1840–49	55s. 11d.	(£2.80)
1850–59	53s. 4d.	(£2.67)
1860–69	51s. 8d.	(£2.58)

from *The Forging of the Modern State* by E. Evans (1983)

0 After Peel's death Joseph Hume set up a Working-Men's Fund, which was used to buy books 'suitable to the working-classes', containing bookplates inscribed like this one
Presented to the Manchester Free Library by the Trustees for the distribution of the Peel Memorial, a fund raised by the Penny Subscriptions of above 400,000 Working Men of the United Kingdom; as a record of their gratitude to the Right Honourable Sir Robert Peel, Baronet, who as Prime Minister in the year 1846, proposed and carried the abolition of the Tax on Bread.

The last words of the speech of Sir Robert Peel,
in the House of Commons on the 29th June, 1846,
announcing the resignation of his Ministry
'It may be that I shall leave a name sometimes remembered with
expressions of good will in the abodes of those whose lot it is to labour,
and to earn their daily bread by the sweat of their brow, when they shall
recruit their exhausted strength by abundant and untaxed food, the
sweeter because it is no longer leavened by a sense of injustice.'

from a bookplate for the Working Men's Memorial of Gratitude

P Even Dickens, whose sympathies were not Conservative, came to admire Peel as a result of the Corn Law crisis
I little thought, once upon a time, that I should ever live to praise Peel,
but Disraeli and that Dunghill Lord [George Bentinck] have so disgusted
me, that I feel disposed to champion him.
At Peel's death Dickens wrote to Harriet Martineau
I am very sorry to see Peel's death in the paper this morning. He was a
man of great importance to the country just now, and could ill be spared
from among the great dust-heap of imbeciles and dandies . . . down at
Westminster.

from letters by Dickens, 3 July 1846 and 3 July 1850

Q It may be no coincidence that one theme of Dickens's novel *Dombey and Son* (begun just after the Repeal of the Corn Laws) is social harmony achieved only after great difficulty. Another theme is the transformation wrought by the railways being built as Dickens wrote. In many respects this passage, which conveys the hope as well as the horror of 'the ringing grooves of change', sums up the age of reform
Louder and louder yet, [the train] shrieks and cries as it comes tearing
on resistless to the goal: and now its way, still like the way of Death, is
strown with ashes thickly. Everything around is blackened. There are
dark pools of water, muddy lanes and miserable habitations far below.
There are jagged walls and falling houses close at hand, and through
the battered roofs and broken windows, wretched rooms are seen,
where want and fever hide themselves in many wretched shapes, while
smoke and crowded gables, and distorted chimneys, and deformity of
brick and mortar penning up deformity of mind and body, choke up the
murky distance. As Mr Dombey looks out of his carriage window, it is
never in his thoughts that the monster who has brought him there has
let the light of day in on these things; not made or caused them.

from *Dombey and Son* by C. Dickens (1847)

Questions

1 To what extent do sources A and M elucidate the motives behind protection in the first half of the 19th century? **(5 marks)**

2 Compare the effectiveness of the rational arguments used in sources C and D with the emotive language used in sources B and E. **(8 marks)**

3 From sources F, G, I, J, K and L select and explain two examples of each of the following types of argument used in defence of free trade: economic; social; moral. **(9 marks)**

4 Compare the responses of sources H and Q to the 'railway mania' of the 1840s. **(8 marks)**

5 To what extent do sources N–P help to explain Peel's popularity after 1846? Which of the other sources in this chapter are helpful in this respect? **(10 marks)**

10 JUDGING THE AGE OF REFORM
THE HISTORICAL DEBATE

This period has attracted a great deal of attention from historians. It has also been the subject of continuing controversy, much of which has reflected the political views of the historians concerned. It is important for students to be able to detect any such bias. They should also be able to use evidence such as has been given in the preceding chapters to make up their own minds about what happened and how to interpret it.

Debate has centred on three major questions:-

1. What were the motives behind reform?
2. How extensive and effective was reform?
3. Was the general improvement in conditions after 1850 due mainly to government action or to other factors?

Varying historical views will be presented in each area of debate; none is conclusive.

1 What were the motives behind reform?

A Kitson Clark argues that reform was part of the spirit of the age

Throughout the reign of Queen Victoria there was in most classes in the country a general tendency towards humanitarianism and reform. It acted with different intensity with different people at different times. Where interest, or ignorance, or prejudice, intervened, it was too often sluggish, or selective, or non-existent. For some who claimed allegiance to it it was no doubt the merest lip-service to a rather loosely conceived ideal. With some it was intermittent, a capacity to be excited by particular revelations or responsive to an organized agitation but not otherwise continuously active. With some it meant absorption in some special social need or abuse, and with some it was a passion for the general welfare of humanity or a clearly conceived social programme. But in whatever form this tendency existed, it helped to give shape to English nineteenth-century history, to secure that on the whole matters were always moving in a particular direction, if they were not always moving very fast.

from *The Making of Victorian England* by G. Kitson Clark (1962)

B Jenifer Hart criticises Kitson Clark's 'Tory' views and claims that reform required effort and commitment

These views are dangerous because they lead imperceptibly to the notion that it is better not to plan: because so much was achieved unplanned, the process can and should be repeated. Unplanned changes are spoken of as 'natural', a praise word. Social progress, it is implied, will take place in the future as in the past without human effort as a result of 'the historical process'. The role of men and of ideas (whether for good or for bad) is belittled: we are, as it were, just drifting at the mercy of chance and of blind forces; but all will turn out for the best because of a generally diffused humanitarianism. The only way of testing the validity of this advice is empirically by examining the evidence offered by the past. And in so far as social reform in nineteenth-century England is concerned, the evidence seems to suggest that most social evils were not removed without fierce battles against absurd arguments, vested interests, obscurantism, and timidity, and that their removal required considerable effort and determination on the part of men . . . who realized that it was worth making a conscious effort to control events. And in this enterprise many of them were assisted, whether they knew it or not, by Benthamism in spite of all its shortcomings . . . in the sense of the humanist notion that the diminution of misery is in itself a sufficient justification for action, and that the reforms need not be justified on the ground that they improve the morality of the sufferer.

from *Nineteenth Century Social Reform* in *Past and Present* (1965)

C E. P. Thompson remains aloof from this debate because he has little respect for any of the so-called 'reformers'

Blue Books [Government Reports] in the early 19th century served many purposes, but reform comes low on the list. Parliamentary investigations took place as a routine response to petitions; as a means of 'handling and channelling' discontent, procrastinating or fobbing off ill-behaved MPs; or purely from an excess of utilitarian officiousness. Ireland's decline through misery after misery to the seemingly inevitable climax of the Great Famine was accompanied by the absence of any important measure of alleviation – and by an average of five Parliamentary inquiries per year. The hand-loom weavers and framework-knitters were duly inquired into as they starved. Eight inquiries in ten years preceded the establishment of the police . . . Mr. Gradgrind was most certainly out and about after 1815 [see Chapter 6 Source Q], but as Dickens knew perfectly well he stood not for an 'awakening of social conscience' or 'sensitiveness to distress' but for efficiency, cheap centralised government, laissez-faire, and sound 'political economy'.

from *The Making of the English Working Class* by E.P. Thompson (1963)

D Eric Evans is also sceptical about the reformers' high-mindedness, arguing that governments had little choice but to reform despite their belief in *laissez-faire*

The industrial revolution, while massively increasing economic growth, created social problems which could not remain unregulated. There was an implicit threat to the established order in an untamed and largely irreligious population freed from the fetters which operated more or less efficiently under the aegis of squire and parson in an eighteenth-century village. This intervention, however, was usually in a permissive or advisory capacity. Local authorities were told what they might do, rarely what they must. Individuals and institutions were encouraged to act, but only rarely did the State accept that it must take the lead if they would not. Above all, the nature of such intervention as was offered suggests that governments believed in the total efficacy only of the free market and self-help.

from *Social Policy 1830–1914* by E. Evans (1978)

E F. M. L. Thompson suggests that from the workers' point of view the motives of the reformers were unimportant.

Many of the working classes perceived the state as simply a source of mischief, or at best as an irrelevance, in their lives, and saw little point or attraction in political activity. Among those in the upper and middle classes who actually wielded authority in the Victorian state there were many who attempted reforms, whether from political expediency or moral purpose, in health, housing, education and working conditions: but their motives were suspect, and their efforts were not greatly appreciated . . . The better-off workers provided for themselves and took pride in not needing or accepting assistance. The poorly paid, the casually employed, and the residuum, for whom most of these measures were designed, resented the interference; this was not unnatural, since the ideal solution which progressive opinion had in mind for them was to remove them from society and pack them off to . . . isolated labour colonies, which happily were too costly ever to get off the drawing board.

from *The Rise of Respectable Society* by F. M. L. Thompson (1988)

2 How extensive and effective was reform?

F Kitson Clark challenges the view, put forward by J. L. and Barbara Hammond during the 1930s, that the first half of the nineteenth century was 'a bleak age'

Very much remained to be done; there were still terribly large slum areas; very bad urban, and for that matter very bad rural, conditions remained everywhere . . . There was much ignorance and a lack of expert help where expert help was desperately desired, and, partly as a result of this, infant mortality stayed at a distressingly high figure. Nevertheless, may it not be said that a corner had been turned? This is a result which should be put alongside the effects of the Industrial Revolution. The great increase of population had taken place, but it had not been necessary to pay the penalties. Instead of men becoming poorer they became richer, instead of life becoming more precarious it slowly became safer. Human beings had been assembled in great masses, and yet the likelihood of death from infectious disease had decreased and . . . was going to go on decreasing.

from *The Making of Victorian England* by G. Kitson Clark (1962)

G E. P. Thompson concludes that if any progress was made the credit for it should go to working-class people themselves
During all this time they were, as a class, repressed and segregated in their own communities. But what the counter-revolution sought to repress grew only more determined in the quasi-legal institutions of the underground. Whenever the pressure of the rulers relaxed, men came from the petty workshops or the weavers' hamlets and asserted new claims. They were told that they had no rights, but they knew that they were born free. The Yeomanry rode down their meeting, and the right of public meeting was gained. The pamphleteers were gaoled, and from the gaols they edited pamphlets. The trade unionists were imprisoned, and they were attended to prison by processions with bands and union banners . . . Such men met Utilitarianism in their daily lives, and they sought to throw it back, not blindly, but with intelligence and moral passion. They fought, not the machine, but the exploitive and oppressive relationships intrinsic to industrial capitalism.

from *The Making of the English Working Class* by E. P. Thompson (1963)

H Norman McCord, discussing the practical difficulties facing the reformers, gives them credit for what they achieved
These years saw the first major reform of the legislature, an eventually fruitful overhaul of local government, significant changes in the structure of the public agencies for the relief of poverty, the beginnings of serious state intervention in matters of education and public health, and the establishment of state agencies of regulation in the fields of education, factories, railways, mines. It was certainly to take a considerable time for these innovations to achieve substantial coverage and effectiveness, but the first steps counted for much . . . By any reasonably practicable standard of human competence and merit – though not of course by standards of Utopian perfection – the period

showed an oligarchy, on the whole well-meaning, reacting with inadequate resources to complex and unprecedented problems. If the context in which they had to operate, and the materials at their disposal, are fully taken into account, it should be possible to spare those who had to take the responsibility for decision-making in that difficult period from some at least of what has certainly been – [in spite of what] Mr. E. P. Thompson [says] – the excessive condemnation of posterity.

from *Some Limitations of the Age of Reform* by N. McCord (1974)

I In his 'revisionist tract' directed against the assumptions of historians like the Hammonds and E. P. Thompson, J. C. D. Clark apparently considers that the reformers achieved too much
In England itself, the effect of the measures of 1828–32 was to open the floodgates to a deluge of Whig-radical reform aimed against the characteristic institutions of the ancien regime. Prime targets were the universities, the public schools, the professions, the armed forces, colonial administration, the civil establishment's patronage machine, the corporations, the old poor law, and the criminal law. A sacred constitution . . . had defended itself with the death penalty. After 1832, the number of capital convictions fell precipitously, and soon capital punishment was confined to a handful of murder cases. The number of clergymen newly appointed to the magistrates' bench fell sharply, and clerical JPs tried dramatically fewer cases. Religion and law were no longer two aspects of the same thing . . . Above all, Whig and radical attack focussed on the Church . . . For a decade, the Church was menaced with disestablishment, a fate which overtook the Irish Church in 1869. A series of less sweeping measures amounted to 'gradual disestablishment' for the English Church.

from *English Society 1688–1832* by J. C. D. Clark (1985)

J Peter Mandler argues that the Whigs, recently disregarded as reformers, paved the way towards progress
Whig governments ruled Britain for seventeen of the twenty-two years between 1830 and 1852 . . . To the reform of political institutions and the extension of political rights – in the long run subversive of aristocratic power – was gradually added a programme of social reforms aimed to demonstrate the practical usefulness and responsiveness of an aristocratic State to popular pressure. In the so-called 'Victorian origins of the welfare state' we can see a more positive and politically effective Whig alternative to the backward-looking appeals which Disraeli and 'Young England' addressed to the old Tory aristocracy to reconnect themselves to the people. For a time, at least, the Whigs did

demonstrate that politics was at least as important to the nation's health and unity as commerce.

from *Aristocratic Government in an Age of Reform* by P. Mandler, (1990)

3 Was the general improvement in conditions after 1850 due mainly to government action or to other factors?

K The Hammonds attribute the ending of 'the bleak age' to a variety of causes

After the forties there was a slow and gradual improvement in the conditions and temper of social life. This was due partly to economic causes. The Repeal of the Corn Laws was followed by a period of growing prosperity . . . The position of the employer was eased, and his risks lessened . . . by the Bank Charter Act of 1844 and the Limited Liability Acts of 1855 and 1862. These conditions undoubtedly made it easier for the great educating forces that were released and inspired by the Chartist movement to bring amenities into social life, and so to modify the sharp separation of classes that distinguished the England of the thirties. The Chartists, wishing to strike at the monstrous inequalities of the age, had pressed for the suffrage, because they thought that the provision of political rights would do for the working classes what it had done for the middle classes. They failed, but the instinct for creating a society out of this chaos was prompting other movements which gained power and emphasis from their agitation. Some of these movements were primarily within the working-class world; others were movements in which all classes co-operated. Between them they lifted the English town out of its first barbarism.

from *The Bleak Age* by J. L. and Barbara Hammond (1934)

L Asa Briggs identifies one of the chief engines of improvement

Quite apart from governmental policy, the inherent vitality of an expanding economy was sufficient to carry the country safely through political storms which made Europe the centre of a series of revolutions in 1848. In particular, railway construction itself, which overshadowed everything else . . . was a stabilizing factor counter-balancing weaknesses in other sectors of the economy and making possible a widening of markets and a lowering of transport costs. The number of passengers carried by rail almost doubled in 1849 when compared with the 1848 figure, and the number of lines open more than doubled between 1848 and 1853. By 1850 . . . the Annual Register could comment without undue optimism that 'the domestic affairs of the

British nation presented a tranquil and, with partial exceptions, a cheering aspect'.

from *The Age of Improvement* by A. Briggs (1979 edn.)

M Boyd Hilton seeks more spiritual reasons for mid-century improvement. He finds them in a change in the image of God 'from that of a fierce headmaster . . . to that of a sort of Santa Claus'
There was a move toward softness, to prevention in place of punishment. The treatment of deviants and social outcasts generally – the poor, the vagrant, the insane, the alcoholic, the child, eventually (though not at once) the criminal – became milder . . . The most obvious development was in the treatment of the poor. The new Poor Law of 1834, with its workhouse test and abolition of outdoor relief, had in theory (though not always in practice) imposed a system of terror and deprivation on the unemployed; by the 1850s the institutions of the Poor Law were being widely used for more generous purposes, for medical and nursing provision and suchlike social kindness.

from *From Retribution to Reform*, an article by B. Hilton (1987)

N Edward Royle says that more secular faiths stimulated improvement
The mid-Victorian period saw the triumph of faith in: the enterprise of active capitalism enabling wealth to be created for the good of all; the virtues of competition and the free-market economy; the morality of individual effort and hard work; the philosophy of utility; the religion of the evangelical; and the politics of the professional and expert.
Royle goes on to show that these ideals were not simply imposed by the bourgeoisie but were independently adopted by the working classes
They were hardly reluctant pupils, and the ideals they seized upon – which can be summed up crudely in the word 'respectability' – arose as much out of working-class pride and traditions as out of the indoctrinating efforts of another class. The leaders of working-class opinion did not accept uncritically the ideals of their economic masters, but found there much with which they could agree: co-operative economics survived within a capitalist framework, mutual improvement served for self-help. Their pride and independence kept them separate from the middle class, and at the same time distinguished them from the labouring poor beneath them.

from *Modern Britain: A Social History 1750–1985* by E. Royle (1987)

O V. A. C. Gatrell argues that the price for 'improvement' was a tightening of the bonds of social control
[During the nineteenth century there was] a mounting disciplinary

assault on those mainly proletarian classes who were assumed to threaten dominant and newly articulated definitions of order: those reluctant to enter a disciplined labour force, for example, or those who were excluded from, or who dissented from, the consensual society which the political nation was beginning to try to construct . . . 'Experts' accumulated evidence that more and yet more bureaucratic control was needed to solve 'problems'. Politicians and public connived in this growth in the interests of reinforcing social discipline in an increasingly fissiparous [divided] society. Law was the means and order the primary objective of this enterprise, and the state became its necessary agent.

from *Crime, authority and the policeman-state* by V. A. C. Gatrell in *Cambridge Social History of Britain* ed. by F. M. L. Thompson (1990)

Postscript

P In a review of José Harris's *A Social History of Britain 1870–1914* the historian, Roy Foster, is struck by the writer's view that modern Britain is
much closer to the pre-1870 period than to the late Victorian and Edwardian era. Today, as in the early 19th century, family structures are pluralist, ramshackle and amorphous; expectation of work is uncertain, personal safety under growing threat; evangelical nostrums [remedies] find a ready audience. Restriction of the role of the state is a topic of furious debate; sinking or swimming seems the rule of the game.
Foster agrees that there is some similarity between
the postmodernist mess of Britain after Thatcher . . . [and] the early-Victorian anarchy denounced by Dickens and Carlyle.

from a review in *The Independent on Sunday*, 4 July 1993

Questions

1 'Some degree of intervention by the State was quite unavoidable.' To what extent is Evans's claim (source D) called into question by the other sources in section 1? **(8 marks)**

2 Do the other documents in section 2 bear out J. C. D. Clark's claim (source I) that the 1832 Reform Act opened 'the floodgates to a deluge of Whig-radical reform'? **(8 marks)**

3 What different explanations do historians give in section 3 for the more stable society which developed after 1850? **(8 marks)**

4 Select two left-wing extracts, two right-wing extracts and two neutral extracts, and explain how the writers' viewpoints are revealed. **(8 marks)**

5 How valid do you find the comparison in source P between late 20th-century and early 19th-century Britain? **(8 marks)**

11

DEALING WITH EXAMINATION QUESTIONS

Specimen Answers to Source-based Questions

Questions based on Chapter 6 – 'Educating the Poor'

Questions

1 To what extent do the experiences conveyed in sources B, C and D help to explain the 1840 literacy rate shown in source A? **(8 marks)**

2 Andrew Bell compared the monitorial school to a steam engine or a spinning machine. How far is this comparison borne out by sources E–H? **(8 marks)**

3 Using sources I–N, evaluate the arguments for and against state educational provision. **(10 marks)**

4 Select from the sources an example of each of the following views and explain each choice in a sentence: utilitarian; *laissez-faire*; religious; secular. **(4 marks)**

5 How far do sources O–Q enable you to judge the extent to which 19th-century educational reformers changed working-class behaviour? **(10 marks)**

Points to note about these questions

1 This question asks you to explain the literacy figure at the beginning of the graph by comparing it with the written sources. Note the words 'to what extent', which indicate that you should consider whether this evidence is sufficient.

2 This question enables you to use some imagination in exploring the aptness of the comparison.

3 To answer this well you should not just sum up the arguments but also consider their provenance and effectiveness.

4 In your explanation try to make the meaning of the word clear.

5 This chapter should have given you some idea of how reformers hoped to change working-class behaviour. The last three sources should be discussed in the light of their aim.

SPECIMEN ANSWERS

1 To what extent do the experiences conveyed in sources B, C and D help to explain the 1840 literacy rate shown in source A? **(8 marks)**

Since couples getting married in 1840 would have received no state-aided elementary education, it is surprising that over 60 per cent of the males and about 50 per cent of the females were able to sign the register. One can assume that a small minority (the upper-class and richer middle-class couples) would have attended public or endowed schools or had private tutors. The written sources suggest ways in which the others could have acquired some literacy. Sunday schools, where they existed, taught many children to read and may thus have helped them learn to write even though, as Hannah More explains, this was not their aim. Bamford and Barker had clearly profited from them and they suggest that others had too. The reports from Manchester and Birmingham bear witness to the varied quality of small private schools in the early 19th century. Lovett's career at such schools suggests that they were not very effective. If the Bamford family's experiences can be taken as representative, many families could not afford them anyway. All these autobiographical writers learnt their basic skills from grandparents, parents or siblings. We can glimpse through them the keen desire for education which existed in some working-class families, but we cannot tell how typical they were. The absence of female accounts accords with the lower female literacy rate; nevertheless we do see girls attending Sunday school and teaching their siblings to read. Altogether the sources demonstrate a haphazard educational provision: many were left illiterate, though the more determined could succeed.

2 Andrew Bell compared the monitorial school to a steam engine or a spinning machine. How far is this comparison borne out by sources E–H? **(8 marks)**

At a time when machines were new and exciting it was common to use them in such similes. Andrew Bell meant this as a favourable comparison; the implication is that the system was efficient, modern and productive. But some contemporaries despised 'steam intellects' and modern readers may also regard a mechanical approach to education as unattractive – human beings are more than just animated computers.

The first three of these sources suggest the regularity and precision of machines. Only the kites hanging from the schoolroom ceiling (F) indicate any sense of freedom. For Frederick Wade (H) economic considerations are paramount, as they would be in a factory, but his approval of the 'softening' of the boys' manners by their 'association with the girls' is evidence of a more humane approach. Thus, on the whole, the sources bear out Bell's point but all show schools as they were meant to be and not necessarily as they were. It is difficult to believe that 19th-century children behaved in such model fashion even under the threat of the cane and the dunce's cap.

3 Using sources I–N, evaluate the arguments for and against state educational provision. **(10 marks)**

The argument used most frequently by Utilitarians and others who wanted the state to provide more education is that it would teach the poor their place in life. They would learn not to be discontented but to carry out their economic functions for the good of all. Society would also benefit from their higher standards of morality and better habits. Although these were persuasive arguments at a time of social unrest, they did not yet convince the majority of MPs that costly state intervention was necessary. They were even less likely to be persuaded by Socialists like Engels, whose main reason for supporting state education was to rid schools of 'the fanaticism of the religious sects' (in which he included the Anglican faith espoused by most MPs).

The arguments on the other side are less cogent than those of the political economists but probably they reflect better the views of ordinary people. Cobbett's prejudice against school-teachers and his resentment at the cost of education to the tax-payer would meet with some popular approval even today. Peel's complacent assumption that education was best funded by private charity was shared by many people of his class – though few were as generous as he was. Baines's fear that the liberties of the people were threatened by state education was widespread, especially among nonconformists. These three passages are representative of the strong resistance to the idea of state education which existed in Britain before 1850. For the time being this point of view prevailed.

4 Select from the sources an example of each of the following views and explain each choice in a sentence: utilitarian; *laissez-faire*; religious; secular. **(4 marks)**

Utilitarianism is exemplified in source I, which argues that education will promote the general good.

Laissez-faire is shown in Peel's assumption in J that private effort is better than public provision.

The religious viewpoint is best reflected in B, which sees the main purpose of education as the inculcation of Christian values.

The most secular view is contained in N, Engels's attack on the 'bigotry' of religious education.

5 How useful are sources O–Q in enabling you to judge the extent to which educational reformers managed to control working-class behaviour? **(10 marks)**

Few of the working-class people whose lives educational reformers sought to control left a record of their experiences. Dickens used his novel *Hard Times* to attack, on their behalf, schools as regimented as the factories and workhouses which he also deplored. The passage quoted both condemns Mr Gradgrind's attempt to bring the circus child into respectable society and suggests that it will fail. While the novel might stimulate the reader's imagination, it reveals more about the writer's feelings than about working-class people. It is more telling when put beside Mayhew's interviews with spirited Londoners, who demonstrate the kind of independence Dickens admired. They cannot be dismissed as 'corrupted and ignorant', even though they had little contact with the moral values of Sir James Kay-Shuttleworth. The costermongers are preoccupied with earning their living and they bring up their children to contribute to the families' welfare. The young flower-girl is proud of the learning she has helped her family to gain and hopes that it will enable her brother, at least, to get on in life. Both Dickens and Mayhew bear out F. M. L. Thompson's plausible conclusion that school had only a limited effect on children's lives. He has drawn on wider evidence than can be presented here, without which questions about social control cannot be fully answered.

Preparing Essay Answers

The reports of the examination boards point out every year that the greatest single weakness among examinees is an inability to respond relevantly. No matter how well read and knowledgeable candidates may be, if they stray too far from the terms of the question they cannot be given credit. Examinations from A Level upwards are basically a test of the candidates' ability to analyse historical material in such a manner as to present a reasoned, informed, response to a specific question. Too often examiners are faced with regurgitated notes on a set of topics, little of which relates to the questions as set. There really is no such animal as an 'easy' exam question at these levels; those who set the papers seldom repeat the exact wording of their questions. This means that each question demands its own individual interpretation. The intelligence and subtlety of the candidates' response will determine how high a mark they score. Examinees must, of course, have 'knowledge', but academic history tests not only what they know but how well they use what they know.

As an aid to the development of effective examination technique, here is a list of questions that candidates should ask themselves when preparing their essays:

1 *Have I answered the questions AS SET* or have I simply imposed my prepared answer on it? (It is remarkable how many exam scripts contain answers to questions that do not appear on the exam paper!)

2 *Have I produced a genuine argument* or have I merely put down a number of disconnected points in the hope that the examiners can work it out for themselves? (Too many answers consist of a list of facts rounded off by the 'Thus it can be seen . . .' type of statement which seldom relates to what has been previously written.)

3 *Have I been relevant in arguing my case* or have I included ideas and facts that have no real relation to the question? (Some candidates simply write down all they know about the topic, assuming that sheer volume will overwhelm the examiner into giving a satisfactory mark. This 'mud-at-the-wall' method is counter-productive since it glaringly exposes the candidate's inability to be selective or show judgement.)

4 *Have I made appropriate use of primary or secondary sources to illustrate my answer?* (Examiners do look for evidence of intelligent reading. Choice, apt, quotation from documents or books does elevate the quality of an answer. Acquaintance with the ideas of modern historians and authorities is a hallmark of the better prepared candidate. However, discretion needs to be shown; putting in quotations where they are not relevant or inserting over-long, rote-learned passages merely looks like padding.)

5 *Have I tried to show originality* or have I just played safe and written a dull, uninspired answer? (Remember, examiners have to plough through vast quantities of dreary, ill-digested material from large numbers of candidates. When, therefore, they come across a script that shows initiative and zest, their interest and sympathy are engaged. A candidate who applies his own reasoning and interpretation to a question may occasionally make naive statements but, given that his basic understanding and knowledge are sound, his ambition will be rewarded. This is not an encouragement to 'waffle' but it is to suggest that, provided always that he keeps to the terms of the question, the candidate is free to follow his own judgements. A thought-provoking answer is likely to be a good answer.)

Possible Essay Titles

1 'The legislation of the Tories between 1823 and 1829 was more genuinely liberal than that of the Whigs between 1832 and 1835.' Do you agree?

The essay should begin with a discussion of what 'liberal' means in this context. The main legislation of the Tories and Whigs should be mentioned and measured against such liberal principles as free trade, the more humane treatment of people, religious equality and the extension of political rights. Thus, for instance, the Tories removed more customs duties but the Whigs removed more capital offences from the statute book. The conclusion must depend on what the student regards as the most fundamentally liberal of these concerns. Those who give high priority to political rights would find it difficult to agree with the title quotation.

2 What were the motives behind the reforms of the period 1833 to 1841?

There is much opportunity for interesting discussion here but it is important to make sure that the essay has a clear shape and plan. One approach would be to describe different possible motives, giving examples of legislation arising from them. Reformers might have been prompted by the desire for political advantage, pressure from radicals, the need to appease the middle class, fear of social disorder, humanitarian concern and Benthamite faith. Of course many measures, like the abolition of slavery or the Poor Law Amendment Act, were occasioned by a variety of motives. It could also be shown that in the later years of Melbourne's premiership the Whigs seemed to be motivated chiefly by the wish to stay in office.

3 Who benefited from the reforms carried out by the Whigs between 1833 and 1841?

A good way of sticking to the question is simply to take different groups of people who may be said to have benefited and discuss how much and how soon they actually gained. They would include children, the poor, slaves, the middle class, nonconformists, even (as E. P. Thompson would claim) the Whigs themselves. This is a chance to assess how effective the Whigs' policies were.

4 How far did the legislation of the Whigs between 1833 and 1841 succeed in overcoming the problems of the time?

The essay should begin by describing the main problems of the time: poor social conditions (especially those resulting from the Industrial Revolution), religious and political inequality, and Ireland. Contemporaries diagnosed these problems in different ways. But political economists, humanitarians and reformers inside and outside parliament were agreed that much needed to be done. Laws dealing with poverty, education, factory conditions, local government, slavery, Dissenters and Ireland should be examined and judged in the terms set by the question. It is difficult, in view of the mounting discontent in the country, to conclude that the Whigs solved all the problems. But they undoubtedly alleviated some of them.

5 Select one reform introduced by the Whigs between 1833 and 1841. Assess its achievements, its limitations and the extent to which it fulfilled its purposes.

The material given in earlier chapters should enable the student to provide enough detailed analysis for an answer. Suitable reforms to choose include the Poor Law Amendment Act, the Factory Act of 1833, the Municipal Corporations Act or (though it is not dealt with in this book) the abolition of slavery. It is important both to describe the measure and to discuss the intentions behind the act. Students should also examine the limitations imposed on it by pressure groups, financial considerations or lack of expertise, and the effects it had (if any) on the area of life which it tried to reform.

6 'It had a sympathetic appreciation of the needs of industrial society.' Discuss this comment on Peel's ministry of 1841–6.

This answer should not just give an account of Peel's ministry. It should also provide a critical analysis of his motives and policies. The 'needs of industrial society' may refer to social problems caused by industrialisation or to the economic requirements of trade and industry. Peel's belief that social problems could be solved if economic requirements were met can be demonstrated with reference to his speeches and measures. Thus it is relevant to discuss not only social legislation (the Factory Act and the Mines Act) but also the acts dealing with banks, companies and railways, the free trade budgets and the repeal of the Corn Laws. How 'sympathetic' Peel was to the people is a matter of opinion: he opposed the Ten Hours movement, for example. But his appreciation of the economic needs of the time is undisputed.

7 'The outstanding politician of his generation.' Do you agree with this assessment of Sir Robert Peel?

This difficult question requires an assessment of Peel's whole career. It should set his achievements against his failures and compare him to other politicians of the day. Students have a good opportunity to reconsider the high opinion Peel has generally enjoyed, perhaps by contrasting him with Lord John Russell whose reputation is arguably due for favourable reappraisal. Peel's work as Home Secretary, his building up of the Conservative party while in opposition and his ministry of 1841 to 1846, should all be examined critically and measured against the judgement given in the title.

8 What, if any, were the differences between Whig and Conservative in the period 1833 to 1846?

A useful beginning would be to mention the Foxite and Pittite origins of the two parties, whose parliamentary representatives still came largely from the same aristocratic class. After Peel's acceptance of the 1832 Act, parliamentary reform was no longer a divisive issue and the parties' attitudes to social reform were not radically different. Greater contrasts can be seen in economic policy, where the Conservatives had a more modern approach, and in religious policy, where the Whigs were more prepared to lessen the power of the Anglican church. Surprisingly (in view of later developments) the Whigs pursued a more aggressive foreign policy under Palmerston than the Conservatives did under Aberdeen. It is relevant to mention at the end that a great realignment in the parties was about to take place.

9 Why were the working-class political movements between 1833 and 1848 generally failures?

It should be made clear from the beginning that there was a great deal of working-class political activity in this period apart from Chartism. Certain aims were dominant: better conditions, political rights, the removal of particular abuses like the exploitation of factory workers. Was it possible for working-class movements to achieve any of this? It is necessary to refer to the reform agitation of 1831–2, to Robert Owen and the GNCTU, to the anti-Poor Law movement and the Short Time Committees, as well as to the Chartists. Then students should indicate underlying reasons for the failure of these efforts, at least in the short term. These failures could be contrasted with the success of the Anti-Corn Law League. And the suggestion could be made that the working class on its own lacked the necessary power and money to challenge governments at this time.

10 Why were the 'hungry forties' followed by a period of 'mid-Victorian prosperity'?

It is appropriate to suggest that these broad descriptions may not be very helpful: the forties were not hungry for everyone all the time and there were still many deprived people in the midst of mid-Victorian prosperity. Nevertheless, reasons can be given for the generally improved conditions after 1850: the social reforms of various governments, the railway boom and its effects on other industries, the removal of trade restrictions, the triumph of middle-class capitalist ideals, even the greater optimism brought about by less stern religious attitudes. The student, like the historian, should decide which to emphasise most.

Specimen Essay Answer

(See especially chapters 7 and 9)

'Peel's budgets did more for the working classes than all Shaftesbury's reforms put together.' How far do you agree with this view?

'Imports and Exports; here is Peel's philosophy! There it begins and there it ends', lamented Lord Shaftesbury in 1842. Peel did not attack his humanitarian fellow-Tory in quite such personal vein, but he opposed as economically inept most of the social reforms which Shaftesbury passionately supported. No two Conservatives differed more radically in what they thought would best answer 'the Condition-of-England question'.

Peel believed that tariffs did more harm than good to trade. Some customs duties had been reduced or removed by governments during the 1820s and '30s but by 1842 they still provided 46 per cent of all government revenue. Peel argued in his first budget speech that these duties not only contributed to the trade slump, with harmful social consequences, but also placed a disproportionate tax burden on the poor. 'Whatever be your financial difficulties and necessities,' he said, 'you must so adapt your measures as not to bear on the comforts of the labouring classes of society.' Peel was convinced that trade would revive so much, once tariffs were reduced, that sufficient revenue would come in despite the lower rates. Meanwhile income tax must be revived, unpopular though it was with the more prosperous sections of the community, including MPs.

A significant section of the Conservative party was unconvinced by Peel's arguments on behalf of free trade – as the split of 1846 demonstrates. Nevertheless he pressed on with the 1842 budget, which reduced many duties and re-introduced tax at 7d in the pound on annual incomes of over £150. The 1845 budget took the process further by abolishing import duties on most raw materials (including cotton), reducing many others (including those on sugar), and retaining income tax. By this time trade had revived, employment had increased, wage levels had risen and working-class discontent had diminished. (Less desirably, perhaps, sugar consumption had doubled.) Peel's last contribution to free trade was his politically disastrous removal of duties from corn in 1846, which was opposed by the protectionists in his own party and followed by his resignation. He remained convinced until his death in 1850 that free trade had contributed as much to 'the happiness of the people' as to 'the accumulation of wealth'.

As a result of his economic policies (rather than his cautious social policies) Peel was a popular hero during the last four years of his life and after his death. To some extent, as Donald Read has shown, he consciously manipulated working-class opinion ('the dumb heart of England', as Carlyle called it) in his anti-Corn Law speeches. His widely quoted resignation speech was particularly effective in this respect. Nevertheless, for all their reappraisal of his achievements in general, historians are still agreed that Peel's free trade budgets were 'the main contribution of governments to the better economic and social situation of the later 1840s' [Derek Beales]. Undoubtedly most working-class people shared in this prosperity.

Shaftesbury (who was, of course, Lord Ashley before 1851) did not vote against Peel's budgets – or, in the end, against the repeal of the Corn Laws. But he was dismissive of such financial measures: 'All Peel's affinities are towards Wealth and capital . . . [to him] cotton is everything, man nothing!' Shaftesbury's own efforts, inspired not by the advice of economists but by Tory-paternalist, Christian concern for his fellow men, were devoted to improving the miserable conditions in which so many of them lived and worked.

Never having set eyes on a factory, he was persuaded in 1833 to lead the campaign in parliament to end child labour in textile mills and to limit the working day of adults to ten hours. The Factory Act of 1833 forbade the employment of children under nine and restricted to 12 the number of hours that could be worked by those under 18. Thus the Ten-Hour campaign continued under Peel's government though the prime minister himself opposed it. He thought that such a reduction in hours would lead to stagnation in trade and hence to hardship for the poor – a well-meaning but mistaken view. Factory Acts were passed in 1844, 1847, 1850 and 1853, all with Shaftesbury's vociferous back-bench support, first in the Commons and, after 1851, in the Lords. As a result textile operatives achieved a standard ten-hour working day, which was later extended to other factory workers.

Meanwhile Shaftesbury had secured the appointment of a Commission to inquire into the employment of children in mines. Its horrifying report struck MPs dumb and the resulting Mines Act of 1842 prohibited the underground employment of children and also of women. Shaftesbury's other main reforming work included a long campaign on behalf of pauper lunatics, the Lodging House Act of 1851 (greatly praised by Dickens), the series of acts which by 1876 ended the use of climbing boys as chimney sweeps (against the opposition of tidy housewives), the setting up of Ragged Schools for 300,000 pupils and his chairmanship of the central board of public health. Carlyle dismissed this long record of public service as 'a universal syllabub of philanthropic twaddle'. Modern historians acknowledge Shaftesbury's faults and mistakes (such as his desire to have all the nude statues at the Great Exhibition covered up), but they accept that without his enormous efforts the abuses he condemned would have continued.

Peel's claim, on his resignation in 1846, was that workers would now be able to 'recruit their exhausted strength with abundant and untaxed food, the sweeter because it is no longer leavened by a sense of injustice'. Shaftesbury's assertion in 1844 was that shortening the hours of labour would give workers 'a time to live and a time to die; a time for those comforts that sweeten life, and a time for those duties that adorn it'. The purposes revealed in these quotations were not mutually exclusive. Both men brought about some sweetening of working-class life, though there is no mode of measurement enabling one to say who achieved more. What neither Peel nor Shaftesbury would concede is that the working classes should be given the political power to seek their own salvation.

BIBLIOGRAPHY

One of the best ways to deepen your knowledge of the early 19th century is to read more of the primary sources quoted in this book. Many of them are easily available as paperbacks or in libraries. The following list contains some of the most readable social and political histories of the period.

Gillian Avery: *Victorian People* (Collins 1970). A sympathetic social history which quotes freely from novels, diaries and letters of the period.

Asa Briggs: *The Age of Improvement 1783–1867* (Longman 1959). This remains essential reading, especially for those interested in social history.

Asa Briggs: *Victorian Cities* (Penguin 1963) Detailed studies of the growing cities of the time – Manchester, Birmingham etc.

John Burnett: *A Social History of Housing* (Routledge & Kegan Paul 1986). A vivid treatment of everyday life.

John Cannon: *Parliamentary Reform 1640–1832* (C U P 1973). A full account of the causes and consequences of Parliamentary Reform.

Anne Digby: *The Poor Law in Nineteenth-Century England and Wales* (Historical Association pamphlet 1982). An excellent brief survey.

Eric Evans: *The Forging of the Modern State: Early Industrial Britain 1783–1870* (Longman 1983). A well-written textbook which gives equal weight to social and political themes and contains a very useful compendium of information.

Derek Fraser: *The Evolution of the British Welfare State* (Macmillan 1978). A clear and full treatment of the topics covered in this book.

Joe Finn: *Chartists and Chartism* (Hodder & Stoughton 1992). A full treatment of all aspects of Chartism (including women), which would make a good companion to this book.

Pamela Horn: *The Rural World 1780–1850* (Hutchinson 1980). A readable account of the changing conditions of rural life.

Michael Ignatieff: *A Just Measure of Pain* (MacMillan 1978). A critical treatment of the 19th-century penal system.

Norman McCord: *British History 1815–1906* (O U P 1991). A particularly clear treatment of most aspects of the period.

Hugh McLeod: *Religion and the Working Classes in the Nineteenth Century* (Macmillan 1984) A short and stimulating survey.

Peter Mathias: *The First Industrial Nation* (Methuen 1969). One of the most readable accounts of the Industrial Revolution.

Donald Read: *Peel and the Victorians* (Basil Blackwell 1987). A study of the relationship between Peel and the general public.

Jane Rendall: *Women in an Industrializing Society 1750–1880* (Blackwell 1990). A Historical Association study which looks at the period from a viewpoint neglected by many conventional histories.

Edward Royle: *Modern Britain: A Social History 1750–1985* (Edward Arnold 1987). A clear and up-to-date social history with a full bibliography.

John Rule: *The Labouring Classes in Early Industrial England* (Longman 1986). A useful perspective on the period which focuses on areas which remain controversial.

Gillian Sutherland: *Elementary Education in the Nineteenth Century* (Historical Association 1971). A succinct introduction to the subject.

A. J. Taylor (ed): *The Standard of Living in Britain in the Industrial Revolution* (Methuen 1975). Contains articles representing various points of view.

F. M. L. Thompson: *The Rise of Respectable Society* (Fontana 1988). A social history organised in themes (work, play, marriage etc).

INDEX

Anti-Corn Law League   5, 8, 82, 87, 93-8, 118

Benthamism   10, 38, 49, 103, 116

Carlyle   14-15, 39, 50, 57, 88-9, 109, 120
Chadwick   38, 83, 87-8
Chartism   5, 6, 8, 13, 20, 39, 45, 46, 77, 82, 107, 118, 122
Church of England   4, 5, 28-37, 60-1, 68, 82, 106, 118
Cobbett   18, 21, 27, 38, 41, 67, 113
Corn Laws   4, 6, 7, 8, 26, 83, 92, 94, 98-100, 107, 117, 120

Dickens   12, 13, 50, 58, 62, 69, 100, 103, 109, 114, 120
Disraeli   14, 89, 94, 100, 106
Dissenters   4, 5, 29-31, 33, 35, 60, 61, 113, 116

Education   5, 8, 15, 36, 50, 58, 60-71, 73, 74, 78, 82, 98, 104, 105, 111-14, 116

Factories   5-8, 9, 11, 14, 16, 51, 61, 72-7, 80, 83, 105, 112, 114, 116-18, 120
Free Trade   5, 92-6, 101, 115, 117, 119, 120
Fry, Elizabeth   32, 49, 50, 54

Gladstone   6, 8, 34, 93
Grey   5, 7, 19, 20, 23, 26

Health Reform   6, 8, 82-91, 104, 105, 120
Howard, John   49, 53-4, 57

Industrial Revolution   4, 9, 12, 72, 104, 105, 116
Ireland   5-8, 29, 30, 32, 33, 93, 98, 103, 106, 116

Kay-Shuttleworth   11, 61, 68, 82, 85, 114

Laissez-faire   10, 15, 71, 93, 103, 104, 111, 113
Liverpool   4-7, 30-1, 92

Mayhew   36-7, 47, 50, 57, 62, 69-70, 79, 114
Melbourne   5, 7, 8, 61, 97, 116
Mines   5, 8, 11, 73, 78-9, 105, 117, 120

O'Connell   4, 6, 7, 29, 33
Oxford Movement   7, 30

Parliamentary Reform   4, 5, 7, 10, 18-27, 28, 50, 82, 106, 110, 117, 118
Peel   4-8, 19, 23, 29, 50, 51, 67, 83, 90, 93-101, 113, 117, 119-21
Police   4, 7, 49, 50, 83, 90, 103
Poor Law   5, 7, 38-48, 49, 82, 83, 88, 106, 108, 116, 117-18
Prisons   4, 6, 7, 19, 24, 49-59, 105

Radicals   10-11, 19, 53, 61, 63, 67, 72, 82, 94, 96, 106, 116
Railways   8, 9, 14, 92-3, 97-8, 100-1, 105, 107, 117, 118
Roman Catholics   4-7, 18-19, 29, 30, 33, 35, 70
Russell   6, 8, 18, 20, 26, 30, 32, 33, 61, 92, 94, 98, 117

Shaftesbury (Ashley)   16, 72, 73, 77, 98, 119-21
Slavery   7, 72, 74, 93, 116, 117

Tory Party   4-8, 24, 29, 49, 52, 72, 92-4, 103, 106, 119
Trade Unions   4, 13, 80, 105

Wellington   5, 7, 18-20, 26, 60
Whig Party   5-8, 10, 17, 18-19, 24, 26, 28-30, 38-9, 49, 52, 61, 67, 72, 83, 92-4, 106, 110, 115-17
Women   20, 28, 39, 41, 45, 46, 50, 52, 54-5, 61, 72-4, 77-81, 89, 120